Why Women Pay More

How to Avoid Marketplace Perils

By
Frances Cerra Whittelsey

Introduction by Ralph Nader

Researcher Marcia Carroll

Center for Study of Responsive Law
Washington, D.C.

Acknowledgments

Marcia Carroll is a diligent and creative researcher. Her long hours of work laid the foundation for this book.

The following people contributed to the production process: Charles Bennington, Jonathan Brown, Julie Gozan, Holley Knaus, Claire Nader, Beverly Orr and Phyllis Turner.

The author also wishes to thank the following people for their support and creative input: Harry Whittelsey, Beth Charas and Eileen McGann.

Some of the material in WHY WOMEN PAY MORE: HOW TO AVOID MARKET PLACE PERILS builds on an earlier work: WOMEN TAKE CHARGE: ASSERTING YOUR RIGHTS IN THE MARKET PLACE by Nina Easton. Copyright © 1983 by Center for Study of Responsive Law.

Copyright © 1993 by Center for Study of Responsive Law

All rights reserved. No part of this book may be reproduced or transmitted in any form or by any means, electronic or mechanical, including photocopying, recording or by an information storage and retrieval system, without the written permission of the publisher, except where permitted by law.

Published by:

Center for Study of Responsive Law
P.O. Box 19367
Washington, DC 20036 Price $10.00

Library of Congress Catalog Card Number: 93-70697

ISBN 0-936758-34-1

Printed in the United States of America.

Printed on 50% Recycled Stock With 10% Post-Consumer Waste

Table of Contents

Introduction

A long cross-cultural tradition of marketplace exploitation of women, where sellers of goods and services overcharge, cheat or damage the health and safety of women, deserves closer scrutiny and correction than the medical community, women's rights groups, consumer associations and the law have provided thus far. Too many merchants of repair, financial and legal services, driven by stereotypes of female flightiness, insecurity, ignorance, and inexperience, are defrauding women. Too many other merchants of medical, pharmaceutical and cosmetic goods and services harm as well as gouge. The relentless drumbeat of advertisements perpetuating these stereotypes or tapping the ingrained vulnerabilities of society's gender discrimination, as in fashion and spousal finances, provides the fertile background for these gender-specific gouges to occur and recur.

Since our report on this subject a decade ago, there has been some progress in awareness among both sellers and women buyers. Some women are asking more questions about certain, unnecessary medical procedures, are seeking out more comfortable shoes, and are developing an interest in learning more about their options in ordering their finances within a marriage or during a divorce proceeding. These initiatives, however, are just scatterings amidst the massive, daily routines of merchants who mistreat women as compared to men simply because they are women. Some of these commercial injustices are episodic incidents created by bad merchants and hucksters. Other injustices are rooted so deeply in stereotypical images and prejudice that they have become full-blown merchandising strategies across entire lines of commerce and industries. Billions of dollars of design and promotion turn these patterns of discrimination into big profits for sellers or modes of exclusion against equal opportunities for women.

Recent trends are in the right direction, to be sure. Glib obfuscations such as "Well, women will pay a lot more than men," "Women are just more emotional, you know, it's just part of being feminine," or "Women can't be expected to know about technical things like cars or plumbing or the law," are less tolerated as excuses for cheating. Moreover, women are moving into the legal and medical professions, as well as other trades, in greater numbers and are sometimes chipping away at long-held biases. And laws are on the books, such as the Equal Credit Opportunity Act of 1974, which give some merchants pause.

Nonetheless, gender-based selling, where none is called for, keeps bouncing back on Main Street, notwithstanding what laws there are or what liberationist attitudes are nominally displayed. Nothing can surpass sharper shopping, questioning and acting to expose and avoid bias in the marketplace. If more women, knowing their rights and equities, individually reject the notion that to have taste means you can be taken, or that insecurities are fair game for a targeted marketing campaign (recall the Virginia Slims ad "You've come a long way, baby,"), then the practice of change becomes widely emulated. Girls begin to learn these wiser ways from their mothers. Mothers can press for more education in the schools as part of existing courses to teach their daughters about this discrimination in the marketplace and how to end it. Billions of dollars of wasteful promotion, poor quality merchandise, unnecessary surgery, drugs and car/home repairs, would be squeezed out of the economy. Greater health, safety, efficiency and peace of mind would be achieved.

As this book, *Why Women Pay More*, by Frances Cerra Whittelsey demonstrates, time and time again sellers will exploit women's vulnerabilities, anxieties and passive self-images as long as they can profitably get away with such practices. But, if they are challenged by the rugged savvy of women taking charge, then sellers will be obliged to win their sales by concentrating more on quality, durability, price competition, safety, truth, competent service and useful product information. Tough shopping tends to alert law enforcement agencies as well; the Food and Drug Administration likely would be more vigilant in safeguarding consumer interests than it has with such products as silicone-gel breast implants, drugs and cosmetics.

Let this book further the fair and competent treatment of women in stores, clinics and hospitals. By using its information to hone their shopping skills, women will be contributing to their own well-being, their children's protection, and the economy's overall quality and prudence.

Ralph Nader
Washington, D.C.
January 1993

Preface

When Ralph Nader asked me to take a fresh look at a book on women's consumer problems, I hesitated briefly because of family and business commitments, and then I knew I had to say yes. Fifteen years of consumer reporting for the *New York Times* and *Newsday* and a lifetime as a feminist had prepared me to tackle what I expected would be a fascinating collection of stories about how women fare in the marketplace.

Yet, I was unprepared for what I found.

I found that women truly do pay more — and get less. All consumers pay more because of unnecessary surgery, but women undergo more unnecessary operations than men do. They go to doctors more and undergo more procedures than men. Yet, when a female and a male are matched against each other in competition for a kidney transplant, women don't get the chance to be free of dialysis as often as men.

Auto insurance rates penalize young people, regardless of individual driving record, but the largest class of people who pay more are women. Women as a group drive less than men, but pay equal rates (except as young adults) when they should be paying about 30 percent less. Insurance rates are supposed to rise as risk rises and the more driving one does, the more exposure one has to the chance of having an accident or damaging one's car. The National Organization for Women has been trying to get its voice heard on the issue, but the insurance industry hasn't even developed a public position on it.

Women pay more to keep up their personal appearances because they are women. Pursuing the image of the thin, ever-young, beautiful blonde, American women pay more for cosmetics and clothes, diet plans and diet foods, face-lifts and body sculpting, than men do. Plastic surgeons have knowingly done procedures to people that could sicken and disfigure them, down-playing the risks and evading faint-hearted law enforcement. Most of the patients of cosmetic surgeons are women.

These were all issues I had written about before, but I had failed to focus on the fact that women bear the brunt of consumer abuse. The insult is triple: women earn less, pay more, and get less.

I also took a look at a "marketplace" I had never examined before: the market where commerce between the sexes takes place. Men and women do business with each other, in this marketplace, primarily via their marriage contract. When these contracts are broken — the average marriage lasts seven years — women generally lose. They bear the major financial burden for raising the children of men who feel free to walk away. Faced with a legal system designed in their favor, most divorcing men get the better of the bargain. Their newly-divorced wives begin a slide that often ends in welfare.

Is this a consumer issue? You bet.

Women pay more for haircuts and dry cleaning because of "traditional" pricing.

Women pay more for auto repairs and used cars and new cars — and African American women pay even more — because the people who sell these services and products believe we are suckers and decide we are the ones on whom they can make their profit margins.

As a feminist, I had focused on women's need for political equality and job opportunities. I had not paid sufficient attention to the fact that women deserve equality in the marketplace, just as they deserve it on the job. Women deserve laws that give them an equal chance to get value for their money and a fair interpretation of the marriage contract.

But legislation won't and can't solve all the problems described in *Why Women Pay More*. One cure for suckerism is to be well-informed. This book, as well as others it suggests for reading, offers information and strategies for defense. We need to hone an informed skepticism so we can see the lies both of the dishonest auto mechanic and the seemingly legitimate cosmetics company that sells water and a few chemicals for the price of hope. We need to recognize the corrupt relationship of women's magazines and the advertisers, and to rely on media like *Consumer Reports* and *Ms.* magazine for objective information.

There are also issues raised in *Why Women Pay More* that women need to talk about, like the negative media images that flood our consciousness. We need to understand that one advertising technique is to find our weak spots and cash in on them, but that good advertising can also help to inform us and support us. Canada has voluntary advertising standards written to prohibit sexist and harmful images of women. The U.S. needs such standards as well. They can be "enforced" by publicizing the findings of independent review boards.

Women need to nurture each other, to stop commenting about pounds lost and gained. Let's turn our measuring gazes on how we can help each other gain strength and overcome the negative influences we've all grown up with.

People can prosper together as equals. When women lose in the marketplace because of abusive practices and a legal system designed to put us at a disadvantage, everyone loses. Economic theory tells us that the market system only works well when buyers and sellers are equally well-informed, and equally able to strike a fair bargain. Otherwise, we end up with inefficiency and waste.

I talked with Gloria Steinem while doing this book, and told her that I was amazed at the pervasiveness of the problems women face. "It's the patriarchy," she explained, matter-of-factly. "Patriarchy," a social system marked by the supremacy of the father, is still with us, although masked by our culture.

Why Women Pay More pushes that mask aside. I hope that the women and men who read it will be motivated to forge the equal partnerships that will bring prosperity for everyone.

Frances Cerra Whittelsey
January 1993

Chapter One

In the Market

There are, after all, times when it is hard to know whether the culprit is racism, sexism and/or plain old suckerism.
Ellen Goodman

Most women spend a lot of time shopping. Some like it, some dislike it, but we all do plenty of it. The jokes that we are spendthrifts are far from the truth — men spend more as a group than women, which is no surprise since they earn $1 for every 74 cents we make.[1]

But the fact is that women can be targets for abuse in the market for "male" goods like cars or car repairs where it has traditionally been held that women have less expertise than men. Furthermore, certain industries have simply charged us more for items and services identical to those provided to men. These "traditional" pricing practices have been going on for so long, in fact, that most women have never even noticed the discrepancy.

Some states and cities, and even individual attorneys, are trying to use consumer protection laws or human rights laws to challenge some of these practices. But the civil rights laws were not written to prevent price discrimination based on gender, and in situations such as bargaining over the price of a car, it seems doubtful that the law will ever be of much help. It is clear that women are going to have to get angry about being played for suckers, and will have to use their buying power to make things change.

Auto Repair

■ "My Hyundai was only six months old, and had about 12,000 miles on it," when I noticed that the clutch needed adjusting," recalled a 39-year-old Long Island woman. "So I took it back to the dealer. When I went to pick it up, the mechanic told me I needed a whole new clutch. I said I didn't see how that could be, that clutches should last a lot longer than 12,000 miles. He said, 'Well, you can drive it if you want, but it's going to go suddenly, and you might be stranded.' I took the car, and made the adjustment to the clutch myself that I originally asked him to do. When the car hit 80,000 miles, I sold it — it still had the original clutch."

■ "A few years ago... my family was traveling across the country in our station wagon," said a 20-year-old college student. "My father had gone to the bathroom and so he was gone when the gas attendant came out to service our car. It appeared that my mother was out-of-state, traveling alone with several children. When the attendant checked the car he told my mother that a serious engine repair would have to be done immediately. When my father came back to the car, the gas attendant retracted his statement."

■ "The [three] repair shops have cost me a lot of unnecessary expense, needless to mention inconvenience, " reported a Florida women. "Finally, with complete disgust, I went to my father to have him look under the hood, to my complete surprise he discovered a loose wire..."

■ "One day I couldn't get in or out of my passenger door because the lock was broken inside," said a 19-year-old women. "As usual I went in and they tore my door apart and fixed the lock, but when they put the door panel on they damaged my speaker and drilled all new holes for it. I approached them and they stated, 'We are not sure it was our men that damaged your speaker and we won't pay for it.' I believe I am being discriminated [against] because I'm only 19."

■ "I brought the car into [the dealer], and they said the problem was that I needed new spark plugs," said a California women. "I said that was impossible since I just had new spark plugs put on only a few days earlier during the regular service check. The mechanic said, no, that indeed I still had the old ones on. I asked if there wasn't a check list they went down when doing service work, a list that matched what was included in my service manual. He said, yes, but they sometimes forget to do things. How often have I paid for things and not gotten what I have paid for?"

■ "[I] brought the problems of the brakes to the attention of the mechanic," said one woman. "He stated he did not notice anything wrong with them. When I left and applied the brakes while coming off of the freeway on my way to work, the brakes continued to shake. Not being a mechanic, I thought I was doing something wrong, maybe I wasn't pushing on the brake hard enough. As time went on, my brakes continued to worsen. I was becoming more and more afraid of driving my car."

Both men and women fall victim to unscrupulous auto repair mechanics. About 40 cents of every dollar spent on auto repairs is spent on fraudulent or incompetent repairs, according to the National Highway Traffic Safety Administration. (As one woman caustically remarked when asked if she had ever been cheated or misled by an auto repair shop: "Who hasn't?")

Women can be particularly vulnerable to fraud because most women still have few opportunities to learn about cars. The Long Island woman, who saved herself the cost of an unnecessary clutch, had a relative who was a car mechanic. She had spent many days observing him, and had learned not only how cars work, but that any reasonably bright person can fix them if she has the right tools. Most women do not have the benefit of such schooling, either formal or informal. When the household tasks get apportioned among the children, its rare for the girls and boys to be given equal opportunity at the dishes and the disk brakes. Few young women sign up for shop courses in auto mechanics, either as self-defense against fraud or as a possible career.

Sherry Rees, who owns a van shuttle service from Tucson to Phoenix, Arizona, became so incensed about being cheated on repairs for her vehicles that she opened her own repair shop. "I was victimized by every auto shop," she said in an interview. "They see you coming. The final straw was when they put a new engine in one of our shuttle vans, and the engine fell off onto the street. They didn't tighten the brackets, and they would not cover the damages."

"I felt I owed it to the females of this community to open a repair shop that caters specifically to women — where they know they won't be ripped off," Rees explained. Her repair shop has been so successful she has had to move three times to bigger quarters. Her business card proclaims,"No More Rip-offs," and then makes plain the market niche she is after. "Automotive Repair Catered to Women, Pick-up & Deliver Available, Open 7 Days." A promise of honesty and convenience — a recipe for success with women buyers today.

Women's ignorance of how cars work, however, should not be over-stressed when it comes to understanding auto repair fraud. The plain fact is that fraud in auto repair is far too common, no matter who's bringing the car in to the shop. Rees, among others, cites the commission-based pay of auto mechanics as a major reason for cheating. The more repairs they do, necessary or unnecessary, the more the mechanics earn. "All my technicians are salaried and work four days a week, 10 hours a day," said Rees.

In 1992, Sears settled a national class action suit that charged that the company's shops performed unnecessary repair work in part because they were paying their mechanics on commission.[2] Sears paid dearly for the bad publicity that resulted, taking a $36.4 million loss in its

Merchandise Group for the third quarter of 1992, compared to a profit of $54.4 million in the third quarter of 1991. Sears reported that its sales of automotive goods dropped about $80 million.[3]

The New York State Consumer Protection Board has suggested that shops be prohibited from paying commission-based salaries to mechanics.[4] Even if this suggestion could be legally implemented, it avoids tackling the problem head-on. New York State, for example, once used State Police Troopers to perform undercover investigations of auto repair shops. Such "sting" operations can result in criminal penalties against repair crooks, threatening them with fines or jail time. Now, New York State uses its motor vehicle department to police auto repairs, and "sting" operations have declined, along with punishment for fraud. A combination of vigorous law enforcement and regular publication of the names of shops with verified complaints would make a much better deterrent than an attempt to control how business owners pay their employees.

Lacking such enforcement, however, women will have to look to themselves for protection.

Bargain Hard to Get That Bargain

A 38-year-old high school political science teacher decided it was time to trade in her old station wagon. The woman, a single mother of two who lives in South Carolina, went to her local Mercury dealer and decided on a Sable station wagon with a sticker price of $16,500. After doing some negotiating, she agreed to buy the car for $14,200.

A few days later, she was with a male friend, and they got to talking about "how tough it is for a single mother to deal in a man's world," the friend recalled. On the spur of the moment, they decided to see if he could get a better deal on the car than she had.

While she waited outside, he went in and pretended to want the very same model station wagon. "I got him down another $800, no sweat," said the friend. "He discriminated against her, and I hate to say it, [I got the better deal] because I'm a guy."

An isolated incident? Apparently not. Women bought 49 percent of all new cars in 1991, up from 36 percent 10 years earlier,[5] and that apparently adds up to higher profits for car dealers. A study done by a Northwestern University Law School professor in 1990 found that white women paid $150 more for the identical car than a white man after they had both gone through a rehearsed process of bargaining. African American men fared worse, paying $400 more, and African American women suffered the most, being offered a price on average $800 higher than the white men.[6]

According to Ian Ayres, the assistant professor who wrote the report, car sales reps are always looking for "suckers," counting on them to boost profits. The average dealer would have made a profit of only $362 on the deals negotiated with white men, but $504 for the deals with white women; $783 for the African American men; and a run-to-the-bank windfall of $1,237 on the African American women.[7]

Note that the study was designed to factor out people's bargaining abilities. The six "car buyers" used in Ayres' study were all college educated, all dressed like professionals, followed a pre-arranged script, and used the same bargaining techniques and even body language. "I expected some differences," Ayres said afterwards, "but nothing as significant as we got. My gut feeling is that bargaining in the United States is inequitable and massively inefficient. It's even more of a problem if it's hurting traditionally disadvantaged groups."[8]

Women faced the same kind of pricing discrimination in their quest for the best price on used cars in a shopping survey done by the New York City Department of Consumer Affairs. Undercover agents went to 50 used car lots, in teams of two. Each asked separately about the same car, after waiting some time between the first and second visits. In an attempt to factor out bargaining ability, they also followed a script.

To their credit, 36 percent of the used car dealers quoted the same price to both men and women. But 42 percent stuck the women with prices that averaged $396.67 higher, while men were quoted higher prices only 22 percent of the time with a price differential of only $183.18.[9]

What went on with the used cars seems to mirror events with new cars: sales reps are looking to make a maximum profit, and will bargain harder against people they stereotype as either less informed or less assertive.

"I think women have to be really well-educated about the cars, and what a reasonable price is," said Nancy Youman, advocate with the New York City Department of Consumer Affairs, in an interview. "Women have to be ruthless, and be willing to walk out if need be — these dealers are looking for suckers."

Some studies have suggested that women are less likely than men to realize that a car sticker price is negotiable. The same may be true for other items like computers, telephone systems, appliances, home improvements, TVs and stereos — the list goes on and on. All these items, and many other products and services, do not, in reality, have a fixed price. Especially in a down economy, when business owners may be desperate to do business, and when many prices are actually dropping due to over-supply and inadequate demand, it is safe to assume that the price for virtually anything — except, maybe, food in a supermarket — is negotiable.

Pet Peeves — That Cost Plenty

I was newly married, and it was the first time I had accompanied my husband, Harry, to buy a suit. We went to the well-known Manhattan store Barney's, which now sells some women's clothes, but at the time catered only to men. Today, Barney's is quite upscale and up-price, but in those days it was competitive with the average department store, if not lower in price.

I was used to ranging through a store, like a Labrador retriever, looking for my hidden quarry trying to find the styles and sizes I wanted. I knew this experience was going to be different when we were met at the door by an impeccably dressed sales clerk who asked my husband what he was looking for. Informed that Harry favored European-cut suits, this gentleman escorted my husband to the proper department, handing him off to the sales clerk there.

Harry did not have to paw through racks of clothes, searching for a design or color he liked, and then the proper size. No, the sales clerk brought things to him for approval. When he was ready to try things on, he was not treated like a potential shoplifter, and told he could only take two or three things at once to the dressing room, only to have to re-dress when he would be ready to try the next items. No, the sales clerk stayed with him, handing him garments as necessary.

Harry settled on a suit, but it didn't fit quite right. There was a crease between the shoulder blades, and the jacket needed more tapering. The waist needed to come in, and the trouser legs, which were unfinished to begin with, had to be hemmed. No problem. Out of nowhere emerged a tailor, chalk and measuring tape in hand. Expertly, he pinned and marked, and ran away with the suit. He did not tell my husband, as I have been told when trying on a blazer or a blouse, to "cuff it up" so the sleeves wouldn't cover his hands. (Obviously, I was born with arms too short.) Nor did he tell him how easy it would be to hem the pants himself (although he actually sews a lot better than I do). No, Harry did not have to pay for the suit and then worry about getting it fixed. It would be ready, perfectly tailored, the next day.

But what really drove my blood pressure up was that there was no extra charge for all this tailoring work. The few women's stores that even offered alterations *always* charged me extra — even when I was buying an expensive suit. I was outraged.

Harry was surprised at my emotional state. This, he informed me, was just about standard treatment for a man buying a suit.

A pet peeve not worth getting excited about? Perhaps, but women are coming to realize that these "little" inequities in the marketplace can really add up. Around the country, both individuals and some consumer protection agencies are taking action on gender-based differences in pricing for haircuts and dry cleaning. And the treasurer of the State of Idaho is waging a one-woman campaign against another bane of women's existence: panty hose that can't be counted on to last a day.

Lydia Justice Edwards decided to see how much her pet peeve was actually costing her. She saved every ruined pair of panty hose for a year: all 130 of them. She totalled up the bill: $520. And she wrote a letter to Ralph Nader as well as to the president of Hanes, her manufacturer of choice:

> The product, whether Hanes or a lesser-known brand, is unreliable, as well as inferior. They may run easily, as we put them on, or they may last through two or three wearings.

> Yes, I'm especially money-conscious: I'm a fiscally-conservative state treasurer. But I can afford this foolishness better than the average woman. What about the young woman today, trying to present a businesslike appearance on $1,000 per month wages, children to support, and a daycare center to pay?

Edwards argues that panty hose are deliberately made so they run easily: a classic case of planned obsolescence. Hanes denies this, insisting in a letter to Edwards, that the company has "experimented with a run-proof garment. However, due to the non-run stitch used in the manufacture of this style, the garment had a thick and unappealing appearance." In short, ugly. Michael Flatow, the President of Hanes, wrote to Edwards that he appreciated her "feedback" and advised her to try opaque tights, which he said were made with yarns that are double or triple the weight of sheer hosiery. Edwards remains unconvinced, believing, she said in an interview, that hosiery makers really know how to make durable, sheer hosiery, but won't — for obvious reasons.

Less open to debate are the accusations that dry cleaners and haircutters charge women more than men for similar, if not identical, services. Dry cleaners were found to charge women 27.3 percent more than men to clean a basic white, cotton shirt.[10] The New York City Department of Consumer Affairs found that two out of three haircutters surveyed charge women 25 percent more than men for a basic shampoo, cut and blow dry. On average, the women paid $20, and men $16.

As you might expect, owners of the hair salons protested that women are fussier than men, and that it takes longer to cut the hair of a woman. Mali Rejaee, for example, who manages the well-known Manhattan salon Kenneth, explained, "For the men, it's always a short haircut and it's in and out. For the women, it's a consultation. They want to talk about the style they want."[11] City investigators, however, were skeptical that hair salon owners had ever bothered to actually calculate their costs. They have certainly never priced their services based on whether someone wants a consultation, a brand new style or just a simple trim.

A Boston hair salon owner, Mario Russo, said he didn't believe any of the rationalizations offered by other owners for the differences in price. "My basic philosophy about men and women is that we schedule just as much time for a man as for a woman. It takes just as much time to do a man's haircut as it does to do a woman's. Most men's cuts are short, but there are just as many details to attend to as a woman's. There's the back of the neck, the sideburns, etc.," Russo told the *Boston Globe*.[12]

Massachusetts now has a law prohibiting gender-based pricing, but a *Boston Globe* survey found 11 out of 20 salons charging women more anyway. The ones charging men and women the same price were found to be either very low-priced, or very high-priced.[13]

The same kind of rationalizations are used by dry cleaners who think it's perfectly O.K. to charge women more than men. Once again, the cleaners protested that women's shirts were really different than men's. Women's shirts don't fit the standard pressing machines, they claimed. But the New York City Department of Consumer Affairs found that very large men's shirts don't fit either. And what about boys' shirts? "It seems appropriate to charge more for *all* shirts that require special attention, but the deciding factor should be based on the shirt of the owner rather than the gender of the owner," concluded the city's report.[14]

As for the issue of free alterations, a few years ago, a California executive got fed up after she was charged $40 to alter a $1,500 evening gown, while her husband received extensive alterations to his tuxedo, free. This woman, Lorie Anderson, and a friend and co-worker, Muriel Kaylin Mabry, who also was charged for alterations at the Saks Fifth Avenue store in Beverly Hills, decided to sue. They enlisted the aid of well-known sex discrimination lawyer, Gloria Allred, who filed a class action suit against Saks.

The suit never went to court. Saks settled, claiming they had done nothing wrong, but had always charged men and women the same price for equivalent alterations. Despite this explanation, Saks eliminated or reduced prices for some alterations to hems, sleeves and waists in its 45 branches nationwide. Anderson and Mabry said, with satisfaction, that the change would save them hundreds of dollars a year.[15]

Taking Charge

Women don't have to quietly put up with price discrimination. If you think you are being charged more than a man for a comparable product or service, you're probably right. Speak up. Take your business elsewhere if the proprietor won't listen. Use your most basic consumer weapon — shop around.

Here are some other general guidelines for getting a fair deal in the market.

■ Be assertive, but try to remain level-toned and calm. Unfortunately, men who raise their voices may be viewed as authoritative, but women who shout may be dismissed as hysterical. Do look the offender in the eye and keep in mind that you are paying this person and you deserve both competency and efficiency.

■ Learn about your home and car. Take courses, read books or have a friend teach you. Simple repairs can be satisfying and fun to do. At the least, you will be able to better protect yourself from fraud; and you will earn a mechanic's respect with your ability to engage in an intelligent conversation about the problem. Using the jargon of the trade will let the mechanic know you are not an easy mark.

■ Be a crafty negotiator. If, after reviewing the estimate for any sort of repair (including the parts or material required, the labor costs and the time required to complete the job), you think the price is too high, tell the person it sounds a little steep and that you are going to shop around some more. A smart contractor or repair shop may bring the estimate down considerably rather than lose business. If you have shopped around, you should have a ceiling figure in mind: go for considerably less than that price in order to reach the desirable figure.

■ Don't let incidents of incompetence or fraud slide. If you are a victim of unfair or deceptive practices, you should lodge a complaint with your city or state consumer protection office.

Home Repair Checklist

Choosing a contractor

■ Check to see if the contractor is licensed if your state requires it, and ask for his or her record. A licensed contractor is no guarantee of great service, but you will have the satisfaction of knowing the person is not running a fly-by-night operation and has something (the license) to lose.

■ If your state has no licensing law, ask the Better Business Bureau about the contractor. Avoid any contractor about which the Bureau has received serious complaints.

■ Referral services, such as Home USA (1-800-466-3872), may provide faster answers about a contractor's record than the Better Business Bureau. These referral services check out a contractor's license, insurance and any customer references. Contractors that pass inspection are included in a registry maintained by the referral service. The service is free to the consumer since the contractor is charged a fee for inclusion in the referral registry. It is a good idea, however, to ask any referral service how long it has been in business and what standards it uses to judge contractors.

■ If possible, ask a friend, who was pleased with some recent work, for the name of the contractor.

■ Ask the contractor you are considering hiring for the names of five or six people in the area for whom he or she has done work; then call those people and ask about the quality of the work, how accurate the initial written estimate was, and whether the contractor responded promptly to any requests for corrections.

■ Don't hire someone who tries to pressure you into signing a contract.

■ Develop contacts with licensed plumbers and electricians on whom you can rely in emergency situations.

■ Make sure the contractor you hire is the one who will do the work; some companies subcontract much of their work.

■ Make sure the company provides liability and compensation insurance to protect you in the event of an accident.

■ If a warranty is offered, read it carefully: Is it "full" (giving the consumer unconditional rights) or "limited" (putting conditions on the rights of consumers)? Does it spell out the terms and conditions in language you understand? Who is responsible for the warranty: the dealer, contractor or manufacturer? What is the duration of the warranty?

Keeping tabs

■ Get written estimates on costs — make sure they include all labor and materials, and any promises that the contractor made orally. Be wary if the contractor insists on open-ended increases. But you should also be aware that written estimates are just that, estimates. Expect some fluctuation in the final price, generally about 15 percent, but make contractors prove their case for the increased costs.

■ Obtain a breakdown of when payments are to be made. Be wary if a contractor asks for a substantial part of the bill before the work is near completion. Find out how much money you lose if you cancel the job.

■ Several days into a major job, ask the municipal permit office to send out inspectors (this is usually done free of charge). Provided the work meets your approval and that of the inspectors, let it continue. If not, have it stopped until changes are made. After completion of the project, request another inspection. Only then should you initiate or complete payment. Never sign anything indicating the work has been completed until you are satisfied with the work.

■ If you are alone in the house at the time a contractor is working, you may want to alert a neighbor or friend. Keep an eye on the workers; know where they are and what they are doing at all times.

Buying a New Car

■ Take the time to comparison shop, and make sure you test drive the cars in which you are interested. You are likely to be taken more seriously as a negotiator if the sales clerk realizes you have shopped around.

■ While the purchase price of your new car is important, don't forget to focus on long-term maintenance costs and the safety of the various models before you choose. *The Car Book*, by Jack Gillis, provides maintenance cost data for cars and details how they fared in crash tests. It also tells you which cars get discounts on insurance, and compares gas mileage.

■ Read reviews of cars, including objective ones published by *Consumer Reports*, available at news stands.

■ Consider a good used car instead of a brand new one. Cars known for their longevity can be a wonderful buy when used. By buying used, you avoid the rapid depreciation of value that occurs with a new car. In addition, a well-made used car, even one with 50,000 miles when you buy it, can outlast a new car.

Make sure you have a trusted mechanic check the vehicle before you close the deal. *The Used Car Book*, by Jack Gillis, is a useful guide for anyone interested in purchasing a used car.

Auto Repair Checklist

Choosing a shop

■ Get recommendations from friends and neighbors on repair shops. In any stable community, the word gets around, not only from customers but from mechanics who will talk about a former boss who condoned or encouraged cheating. If the shop is part of a gas station, consider buying most of your gas there — even if the price is not the lowest in town. The owner will appreciate your loyalty, and is more likely to take special care of your repairs. You can also check your local Better Business Bureau or consumer affairs agency to see if they have unfavorable reports on a particular shop.

■ Another choice is to look for a certified mechanic. The National Institute for Automotive Service Excellence (NIASE) tests and certifies mechanics. Certification is not automatic and an estimated 30 percent of the tests taken are failed. There are about 156,000 mechanics nationwide who are currently certified. But certification in itself is not always a good guarantee.

■ The *Washington Consumers' Checkbook* (put out by the Washington, D.C. Center for the Study of Services) rated Washington-area shops and found little correlation between certification and customer satisfaction.[16] "One explanation for this surprising result," said the *Checkbook's* authors, "is that NIASE certifies only the competence of individual mechanics. Competence of one, or a few, mechanics in one or more service specialties [engine repair, automatic transmission repair, etc.] does not guarantee competence of a shop's other mechanics, much less their diligence and honesty."

■ Shops, rather than individual mechanics, are certified by the American Automobile Association (AAA), which is supposed to inspect for the appropriate equipment and customer conveniences, and examine staffing and quality control procedures. AAA-approved shops offer a 90-day or 4,000-mile parts and labor warranty to AAA members. But again, that certification is not a good guarantee of quality work. "The AAA-approved shops we evaluated," said *Checkbook*, "look better, but only slightly better, than other shops on our quality measure."

■ Keep in mind that only dealers are authorized by their auto companies to perform warranty repairs, but don't ask them to do nonwarranty work until you shop around. It is a good idea to check the independent garages in your area. Unlike dealerships they have nothing to sell except repairs.

■ Some American Automobile Association (AAA) chapters offer a diagnostic service to its members. An AAA mechanic will inspect a car, diagnose its problems, and give the car owner a print-out detailing needed repairs. The mechanic may be able to do the repairs, or the car owner can take the car with the list of needed repairs to another repair shop.

Keeping tabs

■ Learn about your car. Start with the Owner's Manual. Knowing which items need regular periodic maintenance will prevent unnecessary break-downs. Another helpful book is *The Lemon Book*, by Ralph Nader and Clarence Ditlow, which contains essential information on legal remedies for owners stuck with a lemon, along with plenty of other helpful advice on repair problems. But go beyond reading. Go out, look under the hood. Do simple maintenance tasks, like adding oil, yourself. If you have children, encourage both the boys and the girls to take basic shop classes in auto repair.

■ When you bring in your car for repairs, take along a written list of the problems, and keep a copy for yourself. Put this copy in a file, and then, after the repair is done, keep a copy of the receipt. This way, you will be able to track repeat repairs, or those that relate to the same problem. This is essential in building a case that a repair is unnecessary, or that there is a defect in your car that the manufacturer should be covering.

■ When you describe the problem, be as specific as possible. As mentioned earlier, you should describe the symptoms — sounds, smells, feel of car — and when they actually happen (i.e. in cold weather, when the car is stopped, etc.). If you find it difficult to describe, get someone in the shop to go on a test drive.

■ Always get a written estimate before work begins that includes parts and labor, and an estimate of when the work will be completed. Never sign a blank repair order. Cross out the blank lines after the work you request is filled in.

■ Be precise when you order a tune-up. It is a vague term that sometimes means the mechanic will perform a lot of "repairs" you don't need and neglect other items. A tune-up should include a compression check of all cylinders; a check of all engine electrical connections; a check (and often replacement) of ignition points, condenser and plugs; and finally, resetting of all ignition and carburetor adjustments.

Avoiding Marketplace Perils

■ Test drive the car before you pay the bill. Often, it is very obvious that the problems you asked to have fixed still remain.

■ If your suspicions are aroused, don't authorize additional repairs until you have had another diagnosis. Get a written estimate from the second shop, and take it back to the first to see if they will agree to fix the problem at no additional cost.

■ If you pay for repairs that are not done properly, try to get the shop to do the job without additional charge. Speak directly to the service manager (not the service writer who wrote up your original repair order). Ask the manager to test drive the car with you so that you can point out the problems.

■ The Federal Trade Commission suggests using a credit card on auto repairs as a protection against faulty or unnecessary work. If you pay by check, by the time you find out about the problem it may be too late to stop payment. Cash is certainly gone. "According to federal law," says the FTC, "if you have a problem with goods or services purchased with your credit card, you have the same legal rights in dealing with the credit card issuer as you have with the auto mechanic. In other words, because you have the right to withhold payment from the auto mechanic for sloppy or incorrect repairs, you also have the right to refuse to pay the credit card company. Of course, you may withhold no more than the amount of the repair in dispute." (This, however, does not mean that you should willingly accept the demands of merchants that you must use a credit card for a purchase or rental.)

■ If you decide to withhold payment via a credit card, send a letter of explanation, by certified mail, to the shop and the credit card company. If you fail to do this your credit rating may suffer.

■ If your city or state designates an agency to handle auto repair complaints, make use of the agency. Even a less-than-vigorous agency can add leverage to your complaint. Send copies of your complaint letter to everyone who presents even a remote chance of helping, like newspaper action reporters, state or local legislators or the Better Business Bureau.

■ If you are unable to elicit an adequate response from the repair shop, you can bring suit against the facility in small claims court. The fee for filing such an action is small and you generally represent yourself without a lawyer, saving legal fees. Check with your state to find out the dollar limit on claiming damages in small claims court. Your local consumer affairs office, state attorney general's office or the clerk of the court can tell you how to make such a claim.

Other Resources

Auto Repair Shams and Scams: How to Avoid Getting Ripped Off by Chris Harold Stevenson (Price Stern Sloan, Los Angeles, CA, 90048, 1990, $9.95).

The Car Book, by Jack Gillis, (Harper Collins Publishers, New York, NY, 10022, 1993, $11).

The Frugal Shopper by Ralph Nader and Wesley Smith (Center for Study of Responsive Law, P.O. Box 19367, Washington, D.C. 20036, 1992, $10).

The Greaseless Guide to Car Care Confidence, by Mary Jackson (John Muir Publications, Santa Fe, NM 87504, 1-800-888-7504, 1989, $14.95).

The Lemon Book by Ralph Nader and Clarence Ditlow (Moyer Bell Limited, Mount Kisco, NY, 10549, 1990, $12.95).

The Used Car Book by Jack Gillis (Harper Collins Publishers, New York, NY 10022, 1993, $11).

Other Organizations with Valuable Information

Center for Auto Safety, 2001 S Street, N.W., Suite 410, Washington, D.C. 20009. Conducts research on and advocates for highway safety, vehicle safety, economy and reliability and informs citizens of consumer transportation issues.

Consumers Union, 101 Truman Avenue, Yonkers, NY 10703-1057. Provides consumers with information on goods, services, health, and personal finances. Publishes the magazine, *Consumer Reports* (12 issues/$22), and *Zillions*, (6 issues/ $16) a children's magazine offering children tips on nutritious snack foods, movies, books and toys. Also publishes books and newsletters on travel, health, and how to purchase a new or used car.

Buyers Up, P.O. Box 53005, Washington, D.C. 20009. A membership organization dedicated to saving people money through group purchases of heating oil and energy services.

Chapter Two

Health

Before Alice Gilgoff went into labor with her second child, she had planned with her doctor how she wanted her delivery and hospital stay to be handled. There was to be no episiotomy, no shave, no enema, and she and her baby would go home the same day, assuming no complications. But matters didn't work out as planned. As frequently happens, her doctor was not available when contractions sent her to the hospital.

"You don't realize that it is very likely that your doctor won't be there when you go into labor, and that you're going to have to renegotiate when you go to the hospital," Gilgoff says. "I had to bargain in between contractions. I won on the shave, but lost on the enema. And they gave me Pitocin, which I could feel was giving me very unnatural contractions."

After delivery, the hospital refused to allow her to go home without delay, and members of the medical staff paraded into her room to look at this strangely assertive woman. "They really stared at me, asking if I were the one who wanted to go home early," she recalls.

"I had a sore throat by the time I left," she continues. "I felt really sabotaged."

Gilgoff had her next two children at home, with a midwife attending. She calls those experiences "very empowering." Today, Gilgoff is a registered nurse, working in a hospital delivery room in New York City, and is in her last year of training to become a certified midwife herself.

Whether male or female, many people have difficulty communicating their complaints and their feelings to medical specialists. When one is sick, frightened or anxious, and stripped literally of the protective layers we usually have around ourselves, it is hard to question, to bargain or to demand to be treated as an equal partner in the process of medical treatment.

But women have more difficulty with the medical establishment than men. Some women complain that doctors are condescending, that they do not treat their ailments seriously, frequently suggesting emotional causes for physical pains. As in Gilgoff's case, the attitude is one of "doctor (or hospital) knows best," even when the rules being enforced are questionable and seem to be based more on economic and power imperatives than research concerning what is truly beneficial for women.

The practice of medicine, as of any profession, reflects the larger society. The societal stereotypes and biases against women — that they are feeble, less intelligent and more prone to emotional disorders — have tainted the medical profession since its inception.

Ancient Greek physicians developed the theory that the emotional disorder "hysteria" was brought on by the female reproductive system — the word "hysteria" in Greek translates literally as "belonging to the womb." Throughout history male doctors performed hysterectomies and clitoridectomies on women to "cure" mental and emotional disorders.

Just over 100 years ago, a well-known physician, Dr. Issac Ray, argued that all women were likely to fall victim to hysteria, insanity and criminal behavior: "With women it is but a step from extreme nervous susceptibility to downright hysteria, and from that to overt insanity. In the sexual evolution, in pregnancy, in the parturient period, in lactation, strange thoughts, extraordinary feelings, unseasonable appetites, criminal impulses, may haunt a mind at other times innocent and pure."[1]

Now, with women playing a more forceful role throughout society, few would have or publicly express those kinds of thoughts. But the lingering remnants of these attitudes remain — in the doctor who talks down to women patients, who withholds information and who dispenses unnecessary mood-altering drugs. "They think we're short and slight and have high-pitched voices so we must be children," said Dr. Estelle Ramey, an endocrinologist at Georgetown University.

Women consume more health care services than men.[2] They visit physicians more times per year, and receive more services when they do. In fact, even when they report the same type of illness or complaint as men, women undergo more examinations, laboratory tests and blood pressure tests, are given more prescriptions, and are told to come back for more repeat visits. The American Medical Association (AMA), says the reasons for this "are not clear."[3]

Part of the problem, concludes the AMA, may be the lack of research on women's health problems. For example, despite the fact that cardiovascular disease is the leading cause of death in women in the United States,[4] research on this disease has concentrated almost entirely on men. In the case of depression, which afflicts women more than men, research on drugs to combat depression was initially conducted entirely on men.[5] One of the reasons for leaving women out of drug research is that their monthly hormonal rhythms change the effect of drugs — which, of course, is exactly why such studies need to be done. At one point in the month, a woman may actually be over--medicated and at another point, under-medicated.

Although breast cancer strikes one in eight American women, and kills 46,000 a year, it took until 1992 for Congress to budget more than $400 million for research, a three-fold increase from the previous year. Of this amount, $210 million came from the Pentagon's budget.[6] By comparison, the federal budget for the National Institutes of Health is about $10.6 billion for 1993.

In response to the Congressional Caucus for Women's Issues training a spotlight on this lack of research, the National Institutes of

Health (NIH) announced in 1990 the creation of the Women's Health Initiative, a $625 million, 14-year project that will be the largest study ever of diseases in women as they age. The NIH has also created an Office of Research on Women's Health to make sure women and women's health problems are included in NIH-funded studies. By the end of 1992, that office was beginning to fund research on conditions such as the causes of uterine fibroids and endometriosis, common problems whose causes have been largely ignored by researchers.[7] The Food and Drug Administration also now requires drug companies to include women in clinical trials.[8]

As women discovered during the explosive 1992 FDA hearings on the safety of silicone breast implants, much of the medical treatment they receive is not based on good research. There is disturbing evidence that women are subjected to high rates of unnecessary surgery, particularly in the case of hysterectomies and cesarian sections, and that they commonly undergo unnecessary, and potentially dangerous, drug treatment. Women want to know, and need to know, whether estrogen-replacement therapy, tranquilizers and the acne-drug Accutane, to cite some examples, are really safe.

While it will be years before there are clear answers, at least women's needs are now being recognized. As Judy Norsigian, co-director of the Boston Women's Health Book Collective told the journal, *Science*, not long ago, "There has been progress. We're hoping what will change now is that we won't have to stand up on the table and scream to have research done."

While women wait for the results of coming research, it is clear that to protect ourselves we must not be passive consumers who regard doctors as figures with unquestionable authority. We must read, question and assert ourselves with health care professionals, even when it means absorbing stares and ridicule, as Alice Gilgoff did.

Sexist Doctors

Many women feel their doctors treat them like children and refuse to respond to their questions adequately. This complaint is directed primarily, though not solely, at male doctors. "I have encountered two very unempathetic male ob-gyn's," remarked one woman. "One of whom went beyond that to maliciousness."

"I prefer a concerned doctor and those seem to be women doctors," said a 25-year-old administrative secretary. A 53-year-old married woman described women physicians as "more understanding" and men as "more condescending." Studies support the perceptions that female doctors listen better and impart more information. For example, in 1991, researchers audiotaped the interactions between 127 doctors (101 men and 26 women) and 537 adult patients. Not only did they find that the women doctors spent more time with all their patients, both male and female, but also that they talked more, their patients talked more and the talk was more "patient-centered" and skillful in uncovering lifestyle and psychological issues that might be affecting the patients' health.[9] The results of this study, and male doctors' tendency to trivialize women's symptoms, make powerful arguments for using women physicians.

Unfortunately, finding a female physician is not always easy. By 1991, 20 percent of all physicians were female, compared to 15.8 percent in 1983 — an improvement, but still too low a number to make certain that all the women who want to see female doctors can do so.[10]

A professor of psychiatry recalls that when she was a college student she suffered from severe lower back pain during menstruation, and her doctor told her it was all in her head.

A 32-year-old woman learned the hard way what may happen when a doctor ignores a woman's symptoms. While playing volleyball she experienced severe chest pains. "...the pain seemed to radiate straight through my chest and into my back... and it wouldn't go away," she remembers. After calling her doctor several times to complain about the chest pains, she was told that she was just "anxious." The woman remembers being told 'this sounds like anxiety to us' and 'if it continues, please call us.' "And I continued to call," recalls the woman. After experiencing another severe pain attack, the woman went to her doctor's office for an examination. The doctor did a regular resting electrocardiogram, which showed no evidence of a heart attack. Even though the woman displayed classic risk factors for heart disease — she smoked, was overweight, had high blood pressure and their was a history of heart disease in her family — her doctor did not order more aggressive diagnostic tests that would have revealed that in fact she had suffered a heart attack. Finally, three weeks after she experienced the initial chest pains, the woman collapsed in her home and was taken to the hospital where tests confirmed that she had severe coronary artery disease. Tragically, after undergoing heart by-pass surgery, her doctor told her that her heart muscle was so damaged that she had to have a heart transplant.

"Its Only Psychological"

As this woman's experience showed, doctors often treat women's pains less seriously than men's pains, attributing the woman's ailment to emotional distress or psychological disorders. Women, as noted before, do visit the doctor more frequently. "Often men will overlook minor pain while women will go to the doctor for a cure," said Dr. Lawrence Schneiderman of the University of California, San Diego.

Underestimating a patient's complaints can have — and has had — dire consequences. One 53-year-old woman was told her problem was psychological; later, another doctor diagnosed it as a serious physical problem. "If a physician cannot come up with a diagnosis," said one woman, 68, "it is always 'emotional.' After running in circles for almost 15 years, one doctor finally discovered that my thyroid was malfunctioning. Until that time all my complaints were 'emotional.'"

Avoiding Marketplace Perils

A 22-year-old woman from Massachusetts described how she learned the hard way about "doctors who attach labels to symptoms they are not capable of diagnosing." She was having pain in her lower abdomen and visited her doctor. "I complained about severe pain and was told it was psychological," she said. It turned out to be "a blood clot in my uterus that caused me so much pain I could not straighten out my body. A male ob-gyn insisted it was psychological even though I could pinpoint exactly where the pain was located... Serious complications resulted from that neglect."

A 29-year-old woman reported that when she was 21 she had a case of bronchial pneumonia. The doctor she saw first told her: "It's probably in your mind. You probably take after your mother. She's the nervous type too." Another woman's "psychological" lower abdominal pain turned out to be a cyst.

In looking for psychological reasons behind ailments, doctors can go to extremes. One 24-year-old woman reported that her gynecologist gave her a piercingly personal questionnaire before her first visit. The questions asked included:

- How many sexual partners have you had?
- Male or female partners?
- How many partners at one time?
- What is your favorite sexual position?

When the American Medical Association's Council on Ethical and Judicial Affairs took a look at the question of doctors' bias in treating women, it noted that the belief that women are over-anxious about their health may be completely off-base.[11] Noting that women's greater attention to their health may be one reason why they live longer than men, the Council suggested, "Men tend to be *'underanxious'* about their health or to ignore symptoms or illnesses and, consequently, underuse health care."

The Council reviewed studies that show that men are more likely to receive kidney transplants than women, and that cardiovascular disease is not diagnosed or treated early enough in women. With their disease further advanced than men, women die more often than men when they have a first attack, and when they are on the operating table.[12]

The Council concluded that doctors might be choosing men over women for transplant procedures "based on evaluations of social worth or preconceptions about the probable roles of men and women..." They called such conduct "clearly inexcusable," and exhorted physicians to examine their attitudes and practices for bias.

Drugs

Diagnosing symptoms as "emotional" or "psychological" generally leads to prescribing mood-altering drugs. Doctors write about 100 million prescriptions each year for tranquilizers and sedatives, and two-thirds of the recipients are women.[13]

Cynthia Maginniss started taking Valium when she was 16-years-old, just after her mother died.[14] The next several years of her life were a blur. Her gynecologist prescribed Valium when she was depressed and bored as a young housewife. Later he gave her Valium and Darvon for cramps, then Valium during a pregnancy. After the birth of that child, her second, she was depressed and anxious and developed colitis. Her family doctor gave her a relaxant and another painkiller. "My doctors never asked me what else I was taking and didn't tell me what I was being given," said Maginniss.

After experiencing hallucinations and bad dreams, walking into walls and attempting suicide, Maginniss finally sought help from a drug counseling organization, WomenTogether, Inc. of Glassboro, N.J. Her doctors had never warned her about the dangers of the drugs they prescribed, nor did they worry about her addiction. Cynthia Maginniss had become an addict.

Avoiding Marketplace Perils

Millions of women like Maginniss are the victims of what Sidney Wolfe, M.D. calls the "gross over-prescribing of these too-often dangerous drugs." In his book, *Women's Health Alert*, Dr. Wolfe shines a spotlight on the fact that over 2 million American women are taking a sleeping pill or tranquilizer every day for a year or more — far longer than evidence shows is effective or safe. In fact, Dr. Wolfe says, many of the people who use these drugs for more than one or two months will end up addicted and will face serious withdrawal symptoms.[15]

Even at the recommended dosages, he continues, these drugs can often cause many unpleasant and dangerous side-effects, including "confusion, memory loss, poor coordination causing falls and hip fractures, impaired learning ability, slurred speech," and even death.[16] It's a frightening litany, particularly when experts from the World Health Organization agree that these drugs should be prescribed for short-term use only — meaning *less than two weeks*.[17]

Doctors claim that women ask for mood-altering drugs. Some do, of course. But a doctor could say no, and certainly should carefully explain risks and possible side effects. A 68-year-old woman reported that her doctor attempted to push tranquilizers on her to make her "feel good." She wrote: "As a matter of fact one even gave me a free sample and when I asked if this was a tranquilizer, he became very angry and demanded that I just take it, which I did not. In another case, I got a prescription. Again, when I asked what it was, he said I should just take it. It would make me feel good. So I asked the pharmacist, who confirmed my suspicion [that it was a tranquilizer]. Whereupon I tore the prescription to shreds — that made me feel good."

Women's problems with drugs that doctors prescribe go far beyond tranquilizers. Dr. Wolfe contends that "the jury is still out" on whether birth control pills, particularly if used for many years, may increase the risk of breast cancer.[18] In the case of estrogen-replacement drugs, he is far more definite in his opinion, saying, "Female replacement hormones may someday be remembered as the most recklessly prescribed and dangerous drugs of this century."[19] The greatest potential benefit of estrogen, lowering the risk of heart disease, has not been proven, according to Dr. Wolfe, while there is other evidence that long-term use of estrogen doubles the risk of breast cancer. He recommends that only women with severe menopausal symptoms take the drug, and stop before a year has passed.[20]

While the risks of estrogen are often downplayed by doctors and pamphlets found in their waiting rooms, the benefits are not. The makers of estrogen pills promise not only an end to hot flashes and vaginal dryness, but also play up the drug's role in helping to stop the bone loss that can lead to osteoporosis. A pamphlet from Wyeth-Ayerst Laboratories, entitled, *If you've had a hysterectomy*, asks the question, "if your symptoms are gone... why take estrogen?" The answer:

> For example, taking estrogen lessens the chance of breaking a bone... Taking estrogen can lower your chances of breaking a hip or wrist by 50 percent to 60 percent... So, as you can see, estrogen can help you deal with immediate symptoms and, perhaps more important, prevent serious health problems that may not appear for years to come. On the other hand since taking any drug may involve some chance of side effects, estrogen is not right for everybody, so talk with your doctor about it.

Dr. Wolfe points out that lifelong moderate exercise and adequate calcium intake, are a far safer way of preventing osteoporosis. He also advises people over age 70 to minimize their risk of falling by taking such measures as having their vision checked regularly and eliminating hazards in their homes that could contribute to a fall.[21]

Another drug on Dr. Wolfe's list of grossly over-prescribed drugs is Accutane, used for severe cases of acne. He maintains that 10 to 20 times the number of women who should be taking the drug are doing so.[22] Accutane can cause serious birth defects and miscarriages. "The problem," says Dr. Wolfe, "is that too many physicians are prescribing the drug to women who don't need it, and a significant number of these women are getting pregnant."[23] The moral: only take Accutane if your have severe acne, and if you are taking it, do everything possible to prevent a pregnancy.

Infertility Clinics

For women having difficulty conceiving children, hearing about the success of new high tech processes that can help with infertility can inspire feelings of hope. But before submitting to these lengthy, sometimes painful and costly procedures, women need to know just how likely it is that they will conceive.

Unfortunately, obtaining information about success rates may not be easy, and, in fact, clinics may stretch the truth in order to keep business booming. In late 1992, for example, the New York City Department of Consumer Affairs charged one of the city's major hospitals, Mount Sinai Medical Center, with a deceptive trade practice for "exaggerating pregnancy and birth rates at its fertility clinic and failing to substantiate the pregnancy and birth rates it boasted," according to a news release issued by the department.

"With failure rates as high as 90 percent," said the department's commissioner, Mark Green, "it's cruel and deceptive to deprive couples desperately seeking babies of the straight facts." The department noted that U.S citizens spent $2 billion on infertility treatments in 1990, and that repeated attempts at in vitro fertilization — one of the methods known as "assisted reproductive technology" — are often necessary and can cost over $40,000 before a clear cut success or failure is achieved.

How successful are these techniques? According to data gathered from 180 clinics, the live delivery rate for in vitro fertilization was 14 percent; for gamete intrafallopian transfer, often called "GIFT," 22 percent; and, for zygote intrafallopian transfer, 16 percent.[24] All of these procedures involve variations of a process of stimulating a woman's ovaries to produce eggs, retrieving the eggs from the woman's body, and then placing them back into her body at some stage of fertilization or embryonic development.

In the case of Mt. Sinai, the success rate, when calculated by comparing the number of women whose ovaries were stimulated to the number of women who had babies, was 10.9 percent. A Mt. Sinai promotional flyer advertised the success rate as 20 percent.

In a letter to the New York City Department of Consumer Affairs, Barry Freedman, executive vice president of Mt. Sinai, admitted:"...we cannot confirm the overall success rates quoted in the program's materials, and, therefore, these rates should not be presented to the general consumer." In short, buyer beware.

Silicone Breast Implants

Recently, women have been horrified to learn that they were never told about the lack of testing and dangers of silicone breast implants.

Would the estimated 2 million women who opted for breast implants have allowed them if they had known they would mean life-long medical monitoring, at best, and serious, perhaps life-threatening disease at worst? Would they have consented if they had been given the information contained in a May 27, 1992 *Update on Silicone Gel-Filled Breast Implants* released by the U.S. Food and Drug Administration (FDA) 30 years after the implants began to be used? This document, which is a conservative discussion of the risks, tells us:

■ Virtually all silicone implants, including those with their shells intact, "bleed" silicone into the body.

■ The known risks associated with implants include "capsular contracture," a shrinking of the scar tissue that normally forms around the implant. About 40 percent of the time,[25] the implants make the breast hard — for some women, hard as a tennis ball —

painful, and disfigured. Fixing this condition used to be done by painful massaging of the breast, but now it is understood that such massage can make the implant rupture. Therefore, a fix requires major surgery again.

■ Other known risks include calcium deposits and unpleasant changes in sensation in the breast and nipple.

■ Implants can make it harder to detect cancer. Women with implants must be careful to find mammography technicians skilled in x-ray of breasts with implants.

■ An unknown percentage of the implants rupture, spilling silicone into the body. In fact, the life expectancy of the implants is not known, but the FDA says women *should not expect them to last a lifetime.*

These are risks admitted to by the regulatory agency that was supposed to prevent this mass experiment from being carried out on women in the United States. Instead, it took the FDA 10 years to act on its 1982 request for safety data to Dow Corning and the other makers of the implants. Although the FDA stated in 1982 that implants present "a potential unreasonable risk of injury," it took 10 years to get the data from the companies and to reach the conclusion that the companies had not proved the implants safe.[26] In fact, the FDA acted only after intense pressure from the Public Citizen Health Research Group.

Other health experts and public advocates suspect the implants of even more serious risks. The Health Research Group obtained internal Dow Corning and FDA memos in 1988 showing that silicone had caused cancer in 23 percent of animals tested.[27] The FDA's 1992 *Update on Silicone Gel-Filled Breast Implants* notes that questions have been raised as to whether the implants can cause immune-related or connective tissue disorders, such as lupus and scleroderma, which can be fatal.

It also mentions that about 10 percent of the women with implants received a type that is coated with polyurethane foam. This coating, it was found, can break down and release a substance called TDA, which is known to cause cancer in animals. TDA has been found in the breast milk of some women, with unknown consequences for babies who drink the tainted milk.

In the newspaper and television stories that followed revelation of the dangers of the implants to the general public, some women insisted that whatever the risks, they were worth the reward of larger breasts — about 80 percent of implants were used to augment breast size — or the normalizing of their appearance after breast removal due to cancer. Karen, whose story is told in Dr. Wolfe's *Women's Health Alert*, fell into the second category. Her implants were inserted during the same surgery that removed large amounts of precancerous breast tissue.

By the time her final set of implants was removed, she had scars from 10 surgeries, two sets of implants had ruptured, droplets of silicone had migrated throughout her body, she was bleeding and was so tired she could barely walk.[28]

Fortunately, the use of silicone implants has slowed almost to a stop. Now, the FDA requires women who receive silicone implants for reconstructive purposes to be part of an on-going clinical study in which they will be closely monitored for years. According to the FDA's *Update* information, the agency no longer allows women to receive silicone implants for breast augmentation except as part of other clinical studies.

These women will be part of the studies that should have been done long ago. In October, 1992, the *Journal of the American Medical Association* reported the start of the first study "designed to answer basic questions about the safety of silicone gel-filled implants." The study, it said, will attempt to determine "the rate of rupture, infection and contracture."

Most of the manufacturers who so cavalierly produced the implants without care for their female victims have left the business, including Dow Corning. Eager to reassert its good corporate image, Dow has offered to pay $1,200 to any woman who needs implant removal and can't afford it.

But for Dow, and the other manufacturers, the big worry is legal. There are so many lawsuits involving implants that a federal judge is coordinating all the litigation so that documents and testimony can be shared. In addition, attorneys have brought a world-wide class action suit on behalf of all women with implants against all manufacturers.[29]

Unnecessary Surgery

At one time the following so-called "joke" was popular in medical school: Question: What are the symptoms for a hysterectomy? Answer: A Blue Shield card and $200.

The two most common surgical procedures in the United States are hysterectomies and cesarian sections, and the patients, of course, are all women. Doctors have offered up hysterectomies — surgical removal of the uterus — to women as the solution to problems ranging from birth control to backaches. In the case of cesareans, doctors today, dazzled perhaps by their high-tech monitors and out of contact with their patients, are rushing to the knife to deliver babies that would have been delivered vaginally 25 years ago. Too often, the only purpose these major operations serve is to line the doctors' pockets.

A typical example: Dr. Estelle Ramey received a call from a woman who had just been told by her doctor that she had fibroids, small tumors, on her uterus and would have to undergo a hysterectomy. The woman wanted a second opinion. Dr. Ramey gave her the name of a woman physician she knew and trusted, and who was conservative about recommending operations. "It used to be that when they found you had fibroids, they just yanked your uterus," said Ramey. Fibroids are common among women and are usually benign tumors. But doctors often felt that it was easier to remove the entire uterus than to treat the fibroids.

According to figures presented by the Health Research Group in *Women's Health Alert*, about one-quarter of the hysterectomies done each year — 150,000 — are unnecessary. Unless medical practice changes, one in three women in the United States will lose their uteruses by the time they are 60.[30] If the hysterectomy rate in the United States was the same as the United Kingdom or Denmark, 300,000 women in this country would not be subjected to the procedure.

Only about 10 percent of all hysterectomies are performed because of cancerous growths. The rest are "elective" attempts to conquer problems like abnormal bleeding, pelvic pain, benign tumors and overall discomfort and inconvenience.[31] Hysterectomy, according to Dr. Wolfe, "should be the solution of last resort," performed only after treatment with hormones, drugs or even surgery to remove fibroids, not the whole uterus, are tried or considered.[32]

A hysterectomy is necessary in many cases, but it is a major operation and should not be treated lightly. Women who are told they should undergo this operation should always get a second opinion, preferably from a doctor who is conservative about operations, before they undergo the danger, trauma and expense involved.

In the case of cesarian sections, how can the following statistics about laboring women be explained?

> The percentage of babies delivered by cesarean section has grown from 5.5 percent in 1970 to 23.8 percent in 1989.[33]

> Over the past 20 years, there has been a marked increase in the number of women diagnosed as experiencing abnormal labor. At the same time, the cesarean rate for such women has more than doubled, to 73.8 percent in New York State.[34]

The number of babies in "fetal distress" — a decline in the health of the fetus — has also mysteriously grown. Again in New York, cesareans were performed 10.7 percent of the time when this diagnosis was made.[35]

In 1970, only 15 percent of babies in the breech position — delivering feet first, rather than head first — were delivered by cesarean, in contrast to 82 percent in 1986.[36]

Researchers looking for the reasons for these startling changes have noted that the rates for cesareans are highest in for-profit hospitals; that more cesareans occur in metropolitan than rural areas; and that "obstetricians occasionally perform cesarean sections to manage their time, which does represent a form of economic self-interest."[37] Increasingly, it seems that obstetricians have made a habit of doing them.[38]

According to Dr. Wolfe, 50 percent of the 967,000 c-sections done in 1988 were unnecessary, and exposed women to the risks and pain of major surgery.[39]

Woman-Controlled Medicine

Medicine has been so dominated by men in the twentieth century that most women don't realize that it hasn't always been that way. Historically, when it came to having babies, men stepped aside and left the job of helping women in labor to other women called "midwives." Even when women were being systematically denied formal instruction in anatomy and physiology in early Greek civilizations, midwives still handled births.[40]

As the American College of Nurse-Midwives points out, "midwife" means "with woman," and the midwife's role in childbirth can, perhaps, be no better defined than that of being with a laboring woman all through the process, to give support and guidance.

Why Women Pay More

Given the thorough and successful efforts of male physicians to transform the normal process of birth into something dangerous, many women are startled today by the suggestion that it is not necessary to go to a hospital for a normal birth, or that it is not necessary to have a physician assist in the process. Most women accept as routine and necessary — for safety reasons — the high-tech and extremely costly process that almost always accompanies a normal pregnancy. It is a mechanized process of sonograms, intravenous drips and fetal monitoring with labor usually endured while lying flat on one's back. It too frequently ends in cesarean section (as discussed previously) and a lengthy recuperative period.

Is it safer to deliver a baby in a hospital, under the care of a physician, than under the care of a midwife? Statistically, the answer is no, according to a recent study. "Judged by the only two measures of outcome available on birth certificates, birthweight and Apgar scores, mothers and babies have distinctly better than average outcomes when births are attended by midwives, either in or out of hospitals," according to a study of midwifery published in 1992 by the *American Journal of Public Health*.[41] This finding is supported by many other authorities as well. Nurse-midwives, of course, are required to have physician back-up, and refer any woman experiencing abnormal labor to a hospital.

In fact, a safe birth outcome "mainly depends on the mother's good health and the skill and vigilance of her birth attendants," points out the Boston Women's Health Book Collective.[42] Midwives excel at giving women the pre-natal education necessary for good health, and at remaining with their patients throughout labor. Today's midwives are usually registered nurses who have taken one to two years of additional training in obstetrics and gynecology. Most states allow nurse-midwives to prescribe medications, and perform all of the routine procedures of normal gynecological care, such as Pap smears.

By the end of 1993, certified nurse-midwives will be delivering about 5 percent of all babies born in the United States, according to the American College of Nurse-Midwives. Most midwife-assisted births occur in hospitals, although some midwives perform home births or work in free-standing birth centers.

Taking advantage not only of their formal medical training but of the birthing wisdom handed down to them by traditional midwives, nurse-midwives assist women in labor with massage and encourage them to take showers, walk around, stand or crouch on birthing stools. When labor slows, they may use an old-fashioned dose of Castor oil to get things going again, rather than the drug Pitocin, which induces severe contractions.

The contrast with the usual routine in hospital labor rooms, where fetal monitors often chain women to their beds, is sharp. "My picture of being a labor room nurse included time to rub a woman's back, of breathing with them, visualizing with them, helping them with contractions," but that's not the way it is, reports Alice Gilgoff, who is completing her midwife training while working in a major hospital in New York City. "Instead, most of my time [working as a nurse] is spent running from room to room because the monitor isn't running right, or the IV is running out, or I have to give someone Demerol. Birth in a hospital is just not a normal event."

Although hospitals and doctors who fear the competition of midwives continue to set up hurdles to the expansion of midwifery, the national crisis in health care seems certain to accelerate the trend toward more use of midwives. In 1986, the Health Insurance Association of America found that the average cost of a complete package of prenatal and labor and delivery care performed in a free-standing birth center was less than half the cost of a usual delivery in a hospital. Alice Gilgoff reports that some women are being forced to take out bank loans to pay New York City obstetricians who are charging between $5,000 and $10,000 — and want the money upfront — just in case a job lay-off causes the loss of insurance.

Women and AIDS

Women are contracting AIDS at an alarming rate. According to the Center for Disease Control and Prevention, women made up more than 14 percent of the total number of AIDS cases in 1992, up from 11 percent in 1991.[43] In several cities, AIDS is the leading cause of death among women ages 15 to 49.[44] And it is projected that by the year 2000, more than half of all new HIV infections (the virus that causes AIDS) will occur in women.[45]

More disturbing is evidence that women die faster than men after diagnosis and that doctors may overlook testing women for AIDS. According to a 1992 study by the San Francisco Health Department, the median survival time after an AIDS diagnosis was about 11 months for women and almost 15 months for men.[46] According to Gary Cohan, M.D., a member of the medical review board for WomenSearch, an AIDS awareness and medical research group, ..."because women generally are not diagnosed early, they don't have the advantage of getting antiviral treatments. By the time they get to the doctor when they are symptomatic, their immune system is pretty beat up."[47]

One reason women at risk are not tested for AIDS is the misconception that AIDS is not a women's disease. Typical AIDS-related symptoms in women — chronic pelvic inflammatory disease, recurring yeast infections and cervical dysplasia — are unique to women and are missed by many doctors as opportunistic viruses that indicate an AIDS test is in order.

A telephone survey of gynecologists on Long Island also found widespread reluctance to treat women with AIDS. Because infected women are particularly susceptible to invasive cervical cancer, screening for such cancer must be done regularly. Yet only one of 32 private gynecologists contacted agreed to be put on a referral list for women with AIDS.[48]

Dr. Cohan recommends that women be aware of the following:

Avoiding Marketplace Perils

Chronic gynecological infections, as described above, may be a warning sign of immune system dysfunction indicating the possibility of HIV infection.

Unprotected sex is anything short of a condom.

Incubation of the virus can range from five to 15 years.

Men infect women at a higher rate than women infect men.

Women and Smoking

The deleterious health effects of smoking tobacco products are will documented. Smoking causes lung cancer, heart disease and emphysema and has been shown to complicate pregnancy.
Each year, an estimated 3 million smokers worldwide die from tobacco-related diseases. Fortunately, smoking is declining among both men and women.

The tobacco industry loses 2.5 million smokers per year: 500,000 from tobacco related disease, 1 million who quit and 1 million who die from unrelated causes. The cigarette marketers must therefore recruit that many new smokers (called "replacement smokers") each year just to stay even. Since 90 percent of new smokers begin before the age of 18, that means that 90 percent of new smokers are young people. About 3000 youngsters start smoking every day.

Throughout the 1980s, girls initiated smoking at a higher rate than boys. Now, children of both sexes begin smoking at the same rate, and 19 percent of seniors in high school, both boys and girls, are daily smokers. The level of educational attainment is now considered the best predictor of smoking status, including whether or not one will quit. In 1990, 12.3 percent of women with 16 or more years of education smoked, as opposed to 27.1 percent of those with less than 12 years of education. For the next generation, tobacco related disease will fall disproportionately on the poor and unemployed. One reason why women seem to be more likely to continue smoking then men is that women smokers report substantially more concern about weight gain if they quit smoking then men (57.9 versus 26.3 percent).

There is abundant evidence that the tobacco industry targets women and girls in advertising and promotion. The industry makes no bones about hawking "women's brands" of cigarettes, like Virginia Slims, Capri and Eve. In 1990, *The Washington Post* disclosed plans by RJ Reynolds to market a new brand called Dakota, to be aimed at young working-class women. The industry also focuses on the African American community as a valuable — and vulnerable — market, placing billboards in urban neighborhoods, ads in African American publications and giving philanthropic donations to African American organizations. RJ Reynolds was forced to cancel its Uptown brand of cigarettes, aimed at African American women and men, when a wave of community-based protest drew national media attention to the company.

Taking Charge

For years many women failed to question their medical professionals, blindly placing their faith in male physicians, not wanting to know more than what the bills told them.

The situation has begun to change. Some women are switching to female physicians; others are simply equalizing their relationship with male doctors. Some suggestions for establishing an equal relationship with medical professionals include:

■ Look upon your doctor as an employee, not an ultimate authority. For too long the medical profession has been placed on a pedestal, beyond reproach. Medicine is like any consumer service: you pay the bills, you have a right to expect quality.

Avoiding Marketplace Perils

■ Seek out and use women physicians, being careful to check their credentials, such as board certification in their specialty. Studies show they will spend more time with you, will listen better and will give you more information than their male colleagues.

■ If you are pregnant, or need routine gynecological care, give serious thought to using a certified nurse-midwife. Care by a midwife costs less, and will usually yield a more positive birth experience. To locate a certified midwife, contact the American College of Nurse-Midwives at 1522 K Street, N.W., Washington, D.C. 20005, or call (202) 289-0171.

■ Shop around. Like any consumer service, you should make an informed choice about doctors. If you are not satisfied with your doctor, set up an appointment for consultation (not an examination) with another. Dr. Margaret Bridwell of the University of Maryland Health Center advises: "On your first consultation, make sure you are clothed and sitting upright. Often doctors will have you undress and be lying on your back, feet in stirrups, before they will talk to you. That automatically puts you at a disadvantage."

■ Ask questions. If something makes you feel uneasy — you don't see the necessity of a certain operation, you are worried about the side effects of a drug — ask for an explanation. Doctors who have nothing to hide should be willing to explain; if not, it may be a sign that this doctor is not for you.

■ Inquire about a diagnosis or prescribed drugs even if you trust your physician; it can help you become more informed about your health and medical practices.

■ Don't let your physician confuse you with medical jargon. Get an explanation in terms you can understand and explain to your own family members.

■ Describe your symptoms carefully and in detail.

■ Get a second opinion on operations, whether or not you question your doctor's diagnosis. Most insurance companies and health maintenance organizations now require them, anyway.

■ Report improprieties. If you believe your doctor has acted improperly toward you, demand an explanation. If you are not satisfied with the reason, don't let the incident slide. Report it to your state's medical licensing board. It may well be that you are not the only person complaining about the doctor. If the board has enough evidence, it can move against him or her. If not, they will at least be alerted to a potential problem.

■ If you believe your doctor has rendered care to you that is beneath the standard of care you would likely get from other physicians in your community, *and* you have suffered provable damages because of this substandard care, you may wish to sue the doctor for malpractice. Be aware that malpractice suits are difficult to win, because few doctors will testify against other doctors, and because standards of care are subjective. For more information about suing for malpractice, read *The Doctor Book*, by Wesley J. Smith.

■ Start a referral network at your place of employment, school, church, women's group or local club. It is difficult to find the names of good doctors, particularly for women new to a town.

■ If you don't like a doctor's service, let him or her know. Write a letter to the doctor (or clinic or hospital) indicating the reasons for your dissatisfaction and requesting a meeting to discuss problems. You can also not pay the bill. If you do not wish to use that source of medical care again, fine. For many, however, there are few or even no alternatives but to work with the only doctor or clinic in your community. While not paying bills on a matter of principle is a powerful weapon, it is also likely to be so alienating to the professionals that it will make future dealings very difficult, if not impossible.

■ Take more responsibility for your own health. Don't smoke, eat well (avoiding foods with high fat content, salt, and artificial additives) and get plenty of exercise.

■ Become an informed consumer. "To fulfill a collaborative role in all aspects of [your] health-care, education is mandatory," said Catherine Fogel, a nurse from North Carolina.

Breast Implants

■ If you are having any sort of problem with your implant, call the FDA's Product Problem Reporting Program at 1-800-638-6725. Ask for a reporting form to be sent to you. If you wish, all information will be kept confidential.

■ For women who have lost breasts to cancer and surgery, safer alternatives to silicone implants exist. These include saline-filled implants, which have a silicone envelope but are filled with salt water. Manufacturers of these devices have yet to submit safety and effectiveness information, but salt water is natural to the body and is easily absorbed. However, researchers have found rare cases in which the saline can become contaminated with harmful bacteria. In addition, the safety of the silicone envelope is still unknown, and any implant, silicone or saline, impedes mammography.[49] Other alternatives include so-called "flap" surgery, in which tissue, usually from the abdomen, is transplanted; and a prosthesis, the safest of all choices. Y-Me, a support organization for women, has a supply of breast forms available to women who otherwise can't afford them. Contact them at 18220 Harwood Avenue, Homewood, IL 60430, or call 1-800-221-2141.

■ If you have a serious problem with an implant and want to hire an attorney, contact the Public Citizen Health Research Group, (202) 833-3000, for a listing of attorneys who are pursuing litigation against the implant manufacturers.

Other Resources

Breast Cancer and the Environment: The Chlorine Connection (Greenpeace, 1017 West Jackson Boulevard, Chicago, IL, 60607, 1992, no charge).

Dr. Susan Love's Breast Book by Dr. Susan Love, M.D. (Addison-Wesley Publishing, New York, NY, 1991, $14).

The Doctor Book: A Nuts and Bolts Guide to Patient Power by Wesley J. Smith (Price Stern Sloan, 1987), no longer in print but available in libraries.

Eat, Think and Be Healthy! by Michael Jacobson and Paula Klevan (Center for Science in the Public Interest, 1875 Connecticut Avenue, N.W., Suite 300, Washington, D.C. 20009, 1987, $8.95).

Eating Clean: Overcoming Food Hazards (Center for Study of Responsive Law, P.O. Box 19367, Washington, D.C. 20036, 1989, $8).

Every Woman's Health edited by Douglas Thompson (Simon & Schuster, New York, NY 10020, 1993, $14).

Infertility: A Guide for the Childless Couple by Barbara Eck Menning (Prentice-Hall Press, New York, NY, 1988, $10.95).

Lesbians and AIDS—A Bibliography by the Lesbian Herstory Archives (To order, send a SASE to LHEF, AIDS Bibliography, P.O. Box 1258, New York, NY 10116), includes resources applicable to all women.

The New Our Bodies, Ourselves by The Boston Women's Health Book Collective (Touchstone, New York, NY 10020, 1992, $20).

Spinning Straw into Gold by Ronnie Kaye (Simon & Schuster, New York, NY 10020, 1991, $9.95), analyzes the psychological and social aspects of breast cancer).

Avoiding Marketplace Perils

Women's Health Alert by Sidney M. Wolfe, M.D. (Public Citizen Health Research Group, 2000 P Street, N.W., Washington, D.C. 20036, 1991, $7.95).

The Women's Health Data Book (Jacobs Institute of Women's Health, 409 12th Street, S.W., Washington, D.C. 20024-2188, published annually, $24.95), provides the most recent information on such issues as reproductive health, infectious diseases, and mental health.

Worst Pills Best Pills: The Older Adult's Guide to Avoiding Drug-Induced Death or Illness by Sidney M. Wolfe, M.D. (Public Citizen Health Research Group, 2000 P Street, N.W., Washington, D.C. 20036, 1988, $12).

Other Organizations with Valuable Information

Action on Smoking and Health (ASH), 2013 H Street, N.W., Washington, D.C. 20006. Takes legal action for non-smokers' rights and has petitioned government agencies to limit smoking in the workplace and make sure rules are enforced.

American College of Nurse-Midwives, 1522 K Street, N.W., Suite 1000, Washington, D.C. 20005. Provides a nationwide directory of certified midwives, and career information on becoming a midwife.

American Fertility Society, 1209 Montgomery Highway, Birmingham, AL 35216. Offers a list of recommended readings on reproductive health. Publishes an annual directory of fertility clinics and their success rates.

Center for Science in the Public Interest, 1875 Connecticut, N.W., Suite 300, Washington, D.C. 20009. Researches, educates and advocates on nutrition, diet, food safety, alcohol and related health issues. Publishes *Nutrition Action Healthletter* 10 times a year.

The Commonwealth Fund, One East 75th Street, New York, NY 10021. A philanthropic foundation that researches and disseminates information on five major topics: improving health care services, advancing the well-being of elderly people, promoting healthier lifestyles, bettering the health of people of color and developing the capacities of young people.

Gay Men's Health Crisis Network, 129 West 20th Street, 2nd Floor, New York, NY 10011, HOTLINE: (212) 807-6655. The GMHC Hotline staff provides counselling and information to men and women on AIDS and provides referrals to local resources around the country. Information is also available from GMHC's Lesbian AIDS Project (202) 337-3532.

Jacobs Institute of Women's Health, 409 12th Street, S.W., Washington, D.C. 20024-2188. Publishes books and reports on topics affecting women's health, including mammography, surrogate motherhood, and preventive care for older women. Also publishes *The Women's Health Data Book* each year.

National Abortion Federation, 1436 U Street, N.W., Washington, D.C. 20005. Provides abortion information and counselling.

National AIDS Clearinghouse, P.O. Box 6003, Rockville, MD 20849-6003, 1-800-458-5231. Operated by the U.S. Center for Disease Control, the clearinghouse provides information on AIDS and on AIDS clinical trials. Publishes *Facts on Women and AIDS* as well as a nationwide listing of local resources.

National Cancer Institute, Office of Cancer Communications, Building 31, Room 10-A-24, 9000 Rockville Pike, Bethesda, MD 20892,
1-800-4-CANCER. A department of the U.S. National Institutes for Health, NCI operates the Cancer Information Service, providing answers to telephone questions from the general public, patients and their families and health care professionals. Offers printed materials on cancer causes, prevention, detection, treatment and research. Also has listing of resources around the country.

National Women's Health Network, 1325 G Street, N.W., Washington, D.C. 20005. Operates a clearinghouse for women's lifetime wellness. Provides publications on AIDS, cancer, reproductive issues and other women's health topics.

Public Citizen Health Research Group, 2000 P Street, N.W., Washington, D.C. 20036. Advocates public health by monitoring the work of the medical establishment, drug industry and regulatory agencies. Publishes *Healthline* monthly.

RESOLVE, 1310 Broadway, Sommerville, MA 02144, Healthline: (617) 523-0744. This support group for infertile persons/couples publishes a newsletter and provides fact sheets and bibliographies on 60 infertility-related issues. The Healthline provides referrals to doctors across the country and local RESOLVE chapters.

WORLD (Women Organized to Respond to Life-threatening Diseases), P.O. Box 11535, Oakland, CA 94611, (510) 658-6930. WORLD's monthly newsletter about HIV/AIDS is available by subscription. (Call for one free sample.) WORLD also conducts retreats and other activities dealing with HIV/AIDS.

Avoiding Marketplace Perils

Woman's Research & Education Institute, 1700 18th Street, N.W., #400, Washington, D.C. 20009. Researches and disseminates public policy information on issues affecting women, such as family leave, housing, access to health care and women in the military. Publishes *The American Woman*, a series of reports on the current status of women in the U.S.

WomenSearch, 7461 Beverly Boulevard, Suite 304, Los Angeles, CA, 90036, 1-800-64-SEARCH. Provides information on medical research on women and AIDS.

Y-Me Breast Cancer Support Group, 18220 Harwood Avenue, Homewood, IL 60430, 1-800-221-2141. Provides breast cancer counseling and information.

Chapter Three

Finance

More women than ever have jobs outside their homes, but many women, young and old, still do not earn an adequate income. The facts are startling, and need to be blazed into the minds of school-age girls.

■ Two-thirds of all women with children will spend at least part of their lifetimes as single mothers.[1]

■ Forty-five percent of women workers earn less than $6.33 per hour, which is defined as an "adequate" wage by the Institute for Women's Policy Research, based on the government poverty line for a family of four.[2]

■ In 1991, 57.4 percent of women over the age of 16 were in the labor force, compared to 51.6 percent in 1980. Even with day care still hard to find and expensive, 53 percent of mothers with babies less than a year old were in the labor force in 1990.[3]

■ All of this work will not guarantee adequate retirement income for most women. The Older Women's League (OWL) reports that by the late 1980s, women were receiving only 73 percent of the Social Security benefits earned by men, and 58 percent of pension benefits. By the year 2020, OWL predicts, Social Security and pensions will have practically ended poverty among older men, but poverty among older women living alone "will remain widespread."[4]

There are many reasons why women live their lives poorer than men, including: limited access to credit, shoddy treatment by insurance companies and participation in poorly designed retirement programs. With knowledge of their rights, informed shopping and advance planning, women can improve their odds of having adequate financial resources throughout their lives.

Credit

Before Congress passed the Equal Credit Opportunity Act (ECOA) in 1974, financial institutions commonly denied women credit solely because they were women. It was not an accurate or fair way of judging a customer's creditworthiness, of course, but it was an easy way, based on the same stereotypes and myths about women that are rooted elsewhere in the economy.

If a married woman worked outside the home, loan officers would discount all or part of her income in considering the family's credit application. Popular at credit institutions prior to the 1974 Act was the so-called "baby-letter," a physician's statement attesting to a couple's sterility, use of approved birth control methods or willingness to have an abortion. If a woman of child-bearing age could not produce the document, the cost of future children would be taken into account when considering a credit application, and credit was often denied on that basis.

Women with jobs considered "nonprofessional" — such as store clerk, secretary or bank teller — were severely penalized. Less of their income was considered in applying for credit than that of a business executive, nurse or teacher. However, a married woman with any kind of job was considered much more favorably than a single woman. Single women were cast as inherently unstable and incapable of conducting their own affairs. Consequently, creditors were reluctant to grant a mortgage loan to women, and often required a male co-signer.

Avoiding Marketplace Perils

Separated and divorced women faced a different bind. The finances of separated women are often in limbo, and creditors shy away from ambiguous situations. For divorced women, creditors often refused to consider alimony and child support payments as income, even if there were a long history of reliable payments. Often it seemed that just being divorced was cause enough to deny a loan.

In the 20 years since Congress passed the ECOA, credit discrimination against women has not completely disappeared, but it has been greatly reduced. Women have the means to overcome illegal credit practices.

For example, in 1990 The Federal Trade Commission exacted a $50,000 penalty from five affiliated loan companies doing business in Georgia and Texas because they had violated the ECOA. The companies, City Finance Corp. and Walton Loan Co. of Atlanta and the Banner Finance companies in Houston, Dallas and San Antonio, were charged with refusing to consider income from credit applicants who were relying on alimony, child-support, or part-time employment.[5] In a similar case, 10 small loan companies located in Tennessee and Oklahoma were charged with having an illegal policy of requiring credit applicants to be employed full-time.[6]

Barbara Blum, President of Adams National Bank of Washington, D.C. (formerly the Women's National Bank), said in an interview that while blatant sexual bias against women has stopped, more subtle discrimination still occurs. "It has gone underground," she says, "and this will not change until there are women bankers at all levels of banking." Banking is still dominated by white males, Blum reports. At a meeting of the American Bankers Association she had good reason to feel out of place. "I was told the spouses were meeting in another room," she remembers.

Mary Houghton, President of South Shore Bank in Chicago, said in an interview that she believes "white male loan officers have more trouble communicating with women customers than male customers." She added that she believes this is a "generational thing," and that younger male loan officers, who have come into the business since the Equal Credit Opportunity Act has become law, deal more fairly with women.

Your Best Protection: Knowledge

Women who understand their rights under the ECOA, and the standards used by credit institutions for granting credit, have the best chance of obtaining the credit cards, loans or mortgages they need. Every women should try to establish credit in her own name.

In essence, the ECOA outlawed discrimination in all aspects of credit transactions because of sex, marital status, race, religion, national origin, or age (if you are an adult). It applies to all creditors who regularly extend credit, including banks, small loan and finance companies, retail and department stores, credit card companies and credit unions. However, women, like men, have to meet the standards used by lending institutions for granting credit. Some of these include:[7]

■ Your income. Count all sources, not just your job.

■ Debt-payments you are presently carrying. If more than 35 percent of your gross income is presently going to pay your debts, you may be denied.

■ Good credit history. If you have successfully paid back a loan, or have a good record of making payments on credit cards, this is a plus.

■ Roots. Living in the same place for a long time is viewed favorably.

■ Type of job. Professionals and technical jobs rate higher than clerking or unskilled jobs.

Avoiding Marketplace Perils

■ Home ownership.

Under the ECOA, the loan officer may not ask about your marital status, your plans to have children or if you are applying for a separate account not secured by a piece of property. If you are not counting alimony or child support payments as income, then you can't be asked about them. (You can be asked whether you have to *pay* alimony or child support.) However, if you need your alimony or child support income to qualify for the loan, be prepared to prove that you receive it under a permanent court order, not a temporary one, and that you receive your payments regularly.

When rating your credit worthiness, the law prohibits creditors from discounting any of your income because of your sex or marital status, or because it comes from part-time employment, a pension, or a public assistance program.

When you apply for credit, you must be given an answer in 30 days, and if you are rejected, the creditor must specify why you were rejected. A statement such as, "You didn't meet our standards," is unacceptable.[8]

When women get divorced or separated, they sometimes find they can't get credit. This can occur if they changed their name upon marriage and the credit bureau lost their history or, if their joint accounts were reported in the husband's name only. The law, however, requires that when creditors report histories to credit bureaus or to other creditors they must report on both members of a couple if an account is shared, unless the account was established before 1977. If you are married, divorced, separated or widowed, you should check with your credit bureau to ensure that your shared credit history has been reported under your name.

If you believe a creditor has discriminated against you, you should first complain to the creditor. Let the creditor understand that you are aware of your rights. If the creditor won't respond, you can complain to the Federal Trade Commission, the Comptroller of the Currency, the Federal Deposit Insurance Corporation, Office of Thrift Supervision, the National Credit Union Administration or the Department of Justice.

Commonly Asked Questions

Here are some questions and answers about the ECOA based on information from the Federal Trade Commission:

Q. My husband and I have an account that dates back to 1975. How can I make sure that account is being reported in my name?

A. Write to the creditor, giving the account number and the name under which the account is listed, and say that you want the credit history under that account reported in both names. Women should be very careful to identify themselves as "Mary Smith," not "Mrs. John Smith." If you identify yourself as Mrs. John Smith, you will have no credit history because credit bureaus drop off the title and are left with "John Smith and John Smith." "Mrs. John Smith" is a social title, not a legal name.

Q. Aren't separate credit ratings given automatically?

A. Since 1977, yes. Separate credit ratings should be given automatically if you are listed as an authorized user or you are contractually liable (you signed the contract). For example, if a man requests a Sears card, and designates his wife as an 'authorized user,' Sears should report both names.

If a husband requests a credit card and two come in the mail and he gives one to his wife to use as a "courtesy card," or an "authorized user account" she has a right to that credit history.

Q. Is it a good idea to have only these "courtesy" kinds of credit cards?

A. No. If you should divorce, your husband can ask that your name be deleted from the account because the account is really his alone. However, accounts you establish in your own name cannot be cancelled by your spouse if a divorce occurs. The moral: make sure you have at least one account in your own name.

Q. If I am denied credit because of an error in my credit history, what can I do?

A. Write to the credit agency named in the letter denying you credit and request a copy of your credit bureau report. If you find an error, ask the credit agency to investigate — it must, by law. If the agency verifies your report of an error, it must so inform everyone who requested information about you for the past six months. If the agency can't prove you're right or wrong, you are entitled to write a 100-word explanation of the situation that must be included in your credit report.

Q. What happens to my credit if I divorce?

A. When you apply for credit as a divorced woman or widow, you can insist and require that creditors consider the record you shared with your ex-husband.

Q. Will my ex-husband's bad credit rating affect my applications for credit?

A. Women may claim ex-husbands' good credit and they must also claim the bad — unless they can prove why the bad history on the account should not reflect their creditworthiness. For example, if you are separated, live apart, and no longer use the credit card, and your husband has run up unpaid bills on his signatures, you could make a good case for disclaiming his credit history.

Q. Does the ECOA cover business as well as consumer credit?

A. Yes. However a creditor may request information on your marital status. There are also other provisions that treat businesses differently, but which are not impediments to seeking credit.

You will find more ECOA information, provided by the Federal Trade Commission (FTC), in the Appendix of this book.

Insurance

While sex discrimination has been outlawed in the credit industry, gender continues to influence insurance practices. "Classification by gender is not only unfair and burdensome to women, but also it is a largely irrelevant, artificial classification," said Gayle Melich of the National Women's Political Caucus.[9] Melich was testifying at Senate hearings in the early 1980s on proposed legislation that would have outlawed the use of gender as a rating factor in insurance.

After intensive lobbying by the insurance industry, which claimed the change would be very expensive and unfair, the proposal died and remained dormant during the Reagan-Bush years. Nevertheless, in the 1990s, insurers eliminated some practices that disadvantaged women in disability and life insurance, although some abuses still exist. Groups such as the National Organization for Women (NOW) and the National Insurance Consumer Organization (NICO) have continued to study and lobby on the issue. Because insurance rates are decided by each state, women have been pressing their cases in states where the legal and political climate offer some chance of success.

Auto Insurance

Since the days when NOW testified on behalf of an Equal Rights Amendment to the Constitution, it has taken the consistent position that most women are overcharged for auto insurance, including liability, medical and collision coverage. The overcharge has been calculated, on average, to be a whopping 30 percent.[10] How can this be, since auto rates are not based on gender, except in the case of very young drivers? The critical factor, argues NOW, is that the average woman drives less than the average man — about half as many miles per year, at all ages — and has about half as many accidents.[11]

It is not that men, as a group, are worse drivers than women, but that men are exposed to more risk because they drive more. The critical word here is "exposed," because greater exposure is supposed to bring with it higher rates. This fact is recognized by the insurance industry in the way it charges premiums for buses and taxis, but is ignored when it comes to private passenger cars except in the case of young drivers.

Some years ago, Aetna ran an ad which said:

Consider the nearly double crack-up rate of male drivers 25 and under versus female drivers 20 and under. Suppose we at Aetna Life & Casualty ignored this statistical reality. Sister Sue would pay 40 percent more for auto insurance so Brother Bob could pay 20 percent less. Unfair![12]

If we follow this logic, then it is similarly unfair for older women to pay the same premiums for car insurance as men even though they have half the number of accidents.

The proposal here is not to base the premiums on sex. It is to base them on your amount of driving. If you drive more, you should pay more. If you are a woman, and you drive more than average, you would pay more than average. The same for men. Simple. Fair.

Rene Carter, a spokesperson for the American Insurance Association, said in an interview that her organization had "no published position" on a per-mile insurance pricing, and would not comment on the idea.

An industry spokesperson who did not want his name used said that while the idea seems good at first blush, it would be impractical and expensive to put into effect. How, he asked, would you determine how far cars are driven? Patrick Butler, insurance expert for NOW, said in an interview that since it is the car that is being insured, and its odometer is, in reality, its "exposure meter," auditing odometers would be the way to determine annual mileage. Butler acknowledges that there would be some cost for these audits, and that insurers would have to guard against fraud.

However, he emphasized that this system would give consumers control over what they pay for car insurance. "Insurance companies would quote people a per-mile rate based on classification factors, and people could then decide how to use their cars," he said. People who chose to leave their cars at home and use mass transit for shopping trips, for example, would reap an economic benefit instead of paying exactly the same insurance premium as if they had driven their cars. Such a system would reinforce programs designed to discourage driving for environmental reasons, as well.

J. Robert Hunter, head of the National Insurance Consumer Organization, thinks he has a better idea for implementing per-mile insurance rates: make the premiums part of the cost of every gallon of gas. Not only would the problem of fraud be eliminated, so would the problem of uninsured motorists on the road. Other problems remain, however, such as how premiums would be apportioned to insurance companies, and how to even out differences caused by cars that get more miles to the gallon.

One industry official's objection is that per-mile rates would "discriminate against sales people and truck drivers and others who drive a lot and have a good driving record." NOW counters saying that this overlooks the fact that vehicles used for business and commercial purposes are in different rate classes. Also, the industry sees no problem discriminating against all young male drivers, by charging them extra-high rates; or discriminating against all people who live in congested urban areas, no matter how much or how little they drive. Somehow, it is all right to discriminate against all adult women, and charge them 30 percent more than their accident average would dictate, and charge men, of course, that much less.

Avoiding Marketplace Perils

As Patrick Butler points out, "A basic tenet of politics is that an unrepresented group never gets the benefit of discrimination." In other words, women don't yet have the clout to be treated equally. While the logistics of administering a per-mile based insurance system need to be thrashed out, NOW believes the logic and fairness of such a system is inescapable.

Health Insurance

The 1978 Pregnancy Discrimination Act was a giant step forward for women. It required coverage of pregnancy by employee *group* health policies. However, women are still at a disadvantage when it comes to health insurance because how people obtain coverage, and what is covered, are based on men's health needs and working patterns, and not women's.

For example, private, *individual* health policies can still exclude pregnancy from coverage, or can charge women more. Insurance companies rationale for this is that pregnancy is a voluntary condition. That definition, says the National Organization for Women, offers "clear proof that women's experience had no part in shaping either commercial or regulatory policy on an issue profoundly subject to the dictates of a male-dominated society."[13]

Medicare, which provides health care coverage for the elderly, does a better job for men than women for this coverage. It provides more complete coverage for the kinds of illnesses that men experience — so-called "acute" illnesses like lung cancer, pneumonia and prostate problems — than the chronic diseases more commonly suffered by women. These include arthritis, depression and high blood pressure.[14]

Medicare, at least, covers all elderly people, regardless of their work experience or income. That is not true of the private health insurance system that younger people must deal with. Under federal law, part-time workers who work less than 17 hours per week need not be offered the same benefits as full-time workers. Because women constitute the majority of part-time and service workers, they may not have any health insurance at all through their own jobs. For homemakers, there is no health care "group" they can join to receive the benefit of lower group rates. Instead, many women have to depend on obtaining insurance through their spouses.

But the spouse's employer could cut back on dependent coverage, or the woman could end up without insurance because of divorce.[15] Although a federal law called the Consolidated Omnibus
Budget Reconciliation Act (COBRA) requires that a divorced or separated woman be permitted to keep her insurance coverage for up to three years, she is responsible for the premiums. Health insurance premiums are now so high that rarely can one afford them without some input by an employer.

The bottom line is that 14 million women of childbearing age have no health insurance at all, and 5 million have coverage that excludes pregnancy care.[16] More men than women actually have no insurance at all, but this is because more women are receiving Medicaid benefits for pregnancy. Nevertheless, only 42 percent of poor women receive Medicaid, and 33 percent are uninsured.[17]

Pensions & Social Security

Less than one out of ten American families fits the model of male breadwinner, female homemaker and two children. The private pension and Social Security systems are still designed to serve that model family. Here's what the Older Women's League had to say about the subject in its 1990 Mother's Day Report:

Despite significant legislative reforms, fundamental biases against women persist in retirement income programs... As long as women continue to assume greater child and elder care responsibilities, are paid less than men, and live longer, these biases will take an enormous toll on women's retirement income.[18]

Social Security was designed over 50 years ago, so it should come as no surprise that the system does not reflect today's realities. It particularly penalizes full-time homemakers who are divorced. A divorced woman who was married at least 10 years is entitled to receive half her husband's benefit. But the system, set up in the days when divorce was far less common, never intended that she try to live on her 50 percent. Had she and her husband stayed together, they would have received his 100 percent and her 50 percent — a far more liveable situation.

Similarly, married women who work long enough to qualify for Social Security on their own receive only the higher of the benefits to which they are entitled — either their own or their spouse benefit. Thus, although far more women are in the labor force and paying in to Social Security, OWL figures that women will still only get 73 percent of the Social Security benefits that men do since women's pay is still significantly below that of men.[19]

Young widows also face a gap in Social Security. If a woman is widowed at age 40, she must wait until she is 60 (or 50, if disabled) before she begins receiving her spouse's benefit. As Frances Leonard points out in her book *Women & Money*, this gap can leave a widow destitute if she lacks the skills to get anything but a minimum-wage job.[20]

When it comes to private pensions, the picture is even bleaker for women. Only one woman in five over the age of 65 got a pension in 1987, compared to nearly one out of two men,[21] and women are half as likely as men to be employed in positions covered by pension plans.[22] Why? Because, as with Social Security, the system is stacked against women. Here are some of the ways both the Social Security and pension laws work against women:

■ Women's work patterns throughout their lives are significantly different than men's. Women still typically take some years off from paid work to raise children or care for an elderly relative. Pension plans require either five years of continuous work at one job before "vesting," or, begin vesting after three years, with 100 percent vesting after seven years. ("Vesting" is the term used to mean that the money in your pension account actually belongs to you.) Although many U.S. citizens change jobs frequently, women change more often than men, so women are less likely to stay in a job long enough to become vested in their pensions.

■ With Social Security, you need 40 "credits" to qualify for retirement benefits — approximately 10 years of work. (Those born before 1929 need fewer credits.) However, Social Security *benefits* are calculated by a formula that considers your average earnings over your highest 35 years of earnings. Thus, if you worked fewer than 35 years, some years of zero earnings will be included when calculating your average earnings and the size of your benefit. OWL figures that even by the year 2030, fewer than 40 percent of women age 62-69 will have worked 35 years or more, and the remaining 60 percent will have zeros averaged into their earnings record.[23]

■ Type of Employment: More women than men still work part-time, and thus are not covered by company pension plans, or work in service and retail industries that are less likely to offer pensions to anyone. A recent study by the Women's Bureau of the U.S. Labor Department found that 63 percent of women are now working in temporary jobs because they can't find permanent ones.[24]

■ Salaries: On average, working women still earn much less than men: lower salaries mean lower pension and social security benefits.

OWL predicts that the "baby boom" generation, now 20 years from retirement age, will wake up soon and realize how disadvantaged women are by the present design of Social Security and pension plans. The issue, predicts the group, "will become a political hot potato of immense proportions."

Taking Charge

Since the odds are good that a woman will spend at least some of her retirement years alone, all women need to plan and save if they wish to avoid poverty or a much-diminished lifestyle. If you are married, you need to do this planning with your spouse. Books that can help you with detailed planning include: *Our Money Our Selves*, by Ginita Wall, C.P.A., and the editors of *Consumer Reports* magazine; and *Women & Money*, by Frances Leonard. *Your Pension Rights at Divorce*, published by the Pension Rights Center, is very informative and useful even if you have not thought of divorce. It covers the special rules of the federal Civil Service System, military, foreign service, railroad and state and local government retirement systems. You can obtain it for $14.50 by writing to the Pension Rights Center at 918 16th Street, N.W., Washington, D.C. 20006.

Even if you are young, and retirement seems very remote now, you would be wise to consider the following:

■ Find out if your employer offers any kind of pension plan, and whether you qualify for it. If one is offered, make sure you participate. Put something into it each week, even if it is a small amount.

■ If you are single, and your employer does not offer a pension plan, then open an Individual Retirement Account. You can put up to $2,000 a year into an IRA, and that amount will be excluded from your current taxable income.

■ If you don't work, and your husband's employer does not offer a pension, you and your husband can set aside up to $2,250 a year in IRAs. The money can be split any way you like, as long as neither one of you contributes more than $2,000. A fair split depends on your assertiveness in arguing for the value of your labor at home.

■ If you and your husband work and together earn less than $50,000, and his employer offers a pension but yours doesn't, you can put $2,000 a year into an IRA. If your combined income is greater than $50,000, and your husband has a pension, you're out of luck. You are not permitted to have an IRA.

■ If your husband has a pension plan, you must agree in writing to waive survivor benefits. Survivor benefits are what you would receive from the pension if your husband dies. Pension plans let people decide if they want to receive money for as long as they live, or get somewhat smaller payments plus a survivor benefit in the event of death. Get hold of the booklet that explains your husband's plan, and read it thoroughly. If you don't understand it, ask questions.

■ If you are in the midst of a divorce, make sure your spouse's pension plan be considered as part of the settlement. You can bargain for a survivor's benefit, and the private pension plan must honor it.

■ If you are unhappy in your job, but you are close to vesting in your pension plan, stick it out for the extra time. Your pension benefits will be very important to you later in life.

■ Even though Social Security is not designed with women in mind, it is still an absolute mainstay for retirement. To find out where you stand, call your local Social Security Office or 1-800-772-1213 and ask for a "Personal Earnings and Benefits Estimate Statement." With this you will learn the amount credited to your account for each year you worked, and will be able to project your future income.

■ Stay informed about changes in tax laws and laws governing pensions and retirement accounts. Learn about them either by reading the business and financial pages of a good newspaper, or look for bulletins from the Internal Revenue Service at your local library. If you can afford the services of an accountant, use one. A good accountant can be your best friend when it comes to financial health.

Other Resources

U.S. Department of Labor, Pension and Welfare Benefits Administration, Public Affairs Office, 200 Constitution Avenue, N.W., Washington, D.C. 20210. Provides free brochures on pension plans and your rights under ERISA, including *What You Should Know About Pension Law* and *Often Asked Questions About Employee Retirement Benefits*.

Pension Benefit Guaranty Corporation, Office of Communication, 2020 K Street, N.W., Room 7100, Washington, D.C. 20006. Provides free publications on pensions, including *Your Guaranteed Pension* (explains the agency and termination insurance for single employer plans) and *Your Pension* (explains pension rights).

Pension Rights Center, 918 16th Street, N.W., Suite 704, Washington, D.C. 20006. An advocacy organization which provides several publications on pensions including, *Protecting Your Pension Money* ($8), *Can You Count on Getting a Pension?* ($3), *The Pension Plan (Almost) Nobody Knows About* ($3.50), and *Your Pension Rights at Divorce: What Women Need to Know* ($14.50).

EXPOSE (Ex-Partners of Servicemen/women for Equality), P.O. Box 11191, Alexandria, Virginia 22312. Provides information on military ex-partners' rights to benefits, including *A Guide to Military Separation & Divorce* ($5).

NICO (National Insurance Consumer Organization), 121 North Payne Street, Alexandria, VA 22314. Educates consumers on all aspects of buying insurance and serves as a consumer advocate on public policy matters. NICO publications include, *Taking the Bite Out of Insurance: How to Save Money on Life Insurance* ($13.95) and *The Buyer's Guide to Insurance* ($3).

NOW (National Organization for Women) 1000 16th Street, N.W., Washington, D.C. 20036. NOW's Insurance Project provides information and materials on women and auto insurance.

NOW Legal Defense and Education Fund, 99 Hudson Street, New York, NY 10013. Provides an informational resource kit on insurance and pensions for $5. (Note: when ordering kit write "Attention Intake Paralegal" on envelope).

OWL (Older Women's League), 666 11th Street, N.W., Washington, D.C. 20001. A women's rights group that works on health care, employment, pensions and other issues affecting mid-life to older women. Publishes the book, *Women & Money: The Independent Woman's Guide to Financial Security for Life* ($9.95).

For specific questions about your pension plan or a determination of whether your plan meets government standards:

Internal Revenue Service
Employee Plans Division
1111 Constitution Ave., N.W.
Washington, D.C. 20224
(202) 622-6076

Chapter Four

Legal

Place your hopes and dreams in the long future of your marriage; but recognize that the state won't back you in the gamble. When you forego your own career opportunities in the expectation of joint future returns, you place yourself at serious risk; and no amount of bitterness and recrimination will finance you if things don't work out in the end.[1]
Frances Leonard

Throughout his career, Johnny Carson got lots of laughs with jokes about his several divorces. To hear him tell it from the stage of the Tonight Show, his greedy wives were threatening him with poverty despite his multi-million dollar earnings every year. With side-kick Ed McMahon chuckling in the background, Carson succeeded in making himself appear the victim.

Attorney Frances Leonard, whose warning to women planning to marry appears in her excellent book *Women & Money*, knows that reality for most divorced women is far from the picture presented by Carson. Consider Deirdre Akerson, a 44-year-old woman with a graduate degree in political science. Like many other women, she gave up her career plans to raise two children while she was married, for 24 years, to an advertising executive. Hospitalized with injuries she says were inflicted by her husband, she separated from him, but then found herself without any money to support herself.

Her lawyer got the court to order her husband to pay support, but he refused. This meant Deirdre could not pay her lawyer, either. So the lawyer simply abandoned her case, and refused to take the action necessary to collect from the husband. Deirdre lost her home. At one point she lived under a bridge in Florida, and in early 1992, when the New York City Department of Consumer Affairs wrote about her case in the report *Women in Divorce*, she was living in a shelter for the homeless.

According to Deirdre, her lawyer demanded $30,000 to file for a judgment forcing her husband to pay as ordered. The lawyer told her, she recounted, that since she couldn't afford it, she should settle with her husband. "My husband doesn't want to settle — why should he?" Deirdre told Consumer Affairs. "He doesn't pay me anything now. If he settled he'd have to pay me."[2]

Deirdre's case may be extreme, but studies have consistently shown that women are impoverished by divorce. One study found that women's standard of living drops 30 percent after divorce, while men's rise by 10 to 15 percent.[3] Another found the average income of women dropping 16 percent following a divorce, while men's rose 23 percent.[4] While the exact findings of such studies differ, the direction for women is clear: down.

Despite Johnny Carson's complaints, only 15.5 percent of women in 1990 who had ever been divorced were awarded alimony payments, and only 32.3 percent ever received a property settlement. While the Census Bureau did not find much change in the percentage of women getting alimony, it did see a big drop in property settlements, which nearly one of two divorcing women had obtained in 1979.[5] The average amount of money that women older than 40 received in alimony payments for the year 1985 was $4,365, down 24 percent over the previous two years.[6] Children of divorce do not fare well either. The U.S. Census Bureau has found that income available to children drops 37 percent when the father leaves.[7]

Experts who have studied divorce in the United States today believe that the plight of divorcing women has been ironically worsened by what started out as desirable reform. This was the change from divorce laws which required one or the other spouse to prove fault — that the spouse had an affair, for example. Instead, divorce today is no-fault — neither party must prove that there has been some serious breach of the marriage contract. While no-fault divorce stopped many husbands and wives from trying to catch each other in bed, it also had the unintended effect of weakening the bargaining position of women who lack any economic clout of their own.

In the days when a husband had to have grounds for a divorce, a wife who had sacrificed her career in order to support her husband's education and raise the children could bargain for a fair share of his earnings and assets before granting the divorce. Deirdre, for example, would probably have been able to extract alimony and child support payments from her husband in return for granting him the divorce. With no-fault, that weapon is gone, and it has not been replaced by laws or judges who sufficiently recognize the value of many women's contribution to a marriage.[8]

Even under the "equitable distribution" laws operating in most states, judges do not give women a fair share of the husband's earning power, which, as Frances Leonard points out, is the most valuable asset of a marriage. The greatest loss divorced women suffer, she points out, "is the enhanced earning power the husband gained at his wife's expense while she stayed home or otherwise stunted her earning ability and he proceeded apace with his."[9]

OWL, the Older Women's League, believes that alimony, which the group prefers to call "spousal support," should be considered delayed compensation for the "sacrifice of earning potential by the homemaker or low-wage employed wife." Or, it could be thought of as unemployment insurance to an involuntarily laid-off employee, the wife. OWL sees spousal support as justice for the wife because, "An unpaid homemaking career combined with age and sex discrimination can amount to permanent employment disqualification for mid-life and older divorced women."[10]

Obviously, this point of view is not generally accepted. Because divorce law does not automatically give value to many women's contributions to a marriage, women need the best legal representation possible to obtain a fair settlement. Unfortunately, it is often not available to them. Either they can't afford it, or, too often, the expensive lawyers they do hire fail them miserably. Gender bias is still common throughout the legal system, and affects women significantly when they interact with it in matters of child custody, protection against violent spouses, and other aspects of family law.

What Price Justice?

Equitable distribution laws had another effect which women did not expect: it dramatically drove up the cost of divorce. In New York, before 1980 when the law went into effect, a contested divorce cost about $6,000. Today, the price tag is $50,000.[11]

The inside joke among New York lawyers, in fact, is that equitable distribution is an ERA for lawyers, with "ERA" not meaning "Equal Rights Amendment," but "Economic Recovery Act" for appraisers, accountants and lawyers, according to Court Referee Steve Liebman.[12]

The reason why the law became a windfall for lawyers is that "equitable" does not mean equal, as it has been interpreted. "Equitable" does not mean that everything is split fifty-fifty. The contending lawyers try to locate all the assets of a marriage, and than evaluate them, arguing over the rights of each party to them. Unscrupulous lawyers feel free to indulge their greed, and, as Whitney North Seymour Jr. wrote in a letter to New York City Consumer Affairs Commissioner Mark Green, "lawyer greed is perfectly legal."[13]

In its devastating report called, *Women in Divorce*, which was based on 107 interviews with lawyers, divorce clients, legal scholars and judges, the New York City Department of Consumer Affairs found a series of abuses which collectively add up to an urgent need for reform. Among them were:

■ Hourly billing by lawyers, the usual fee method, encourages lawyers to delay settlements so their fees increase.

■ In order to collect their fees from women clients, lawyers have put liens on their homes, seized their retirement accounts and anything else they can grab. Their lack of vigor in pursuing husbands, without large fees paid up front, stands in sharp contrast to this collection blitz against their women clients.

■ Attorneys too often help male clients to conceal assets, illegal behavior that is rarely, if ever, prosecuted.

■ Lawyers will often pressure women clients to settle prematurely, using the prospect of enormous fees if they press the case to persuade them to give up.

■ Lawyers often will take large fees and then do little work to advance the case.

In Deirdre's case, her lawyer abandoned her because she could not come up with his fee. Like other women across the country, she then had nowhere to turn for legal help. She could not qualify for free legal services from the federally funded Legal Services Corporation because her husband's income was too high. Even private law firms and clinics that use a sliding fee scale, adjusting their bills to a client's income, generally base their fees on family income, not what is available to the woman. Technically she was in the middle to upper middle income bracket; in reality she was in poverty.

The problem affects not only wives without jobs, but women with full-time jobs as well because the cost of attorneys has become so high. "For anybody with a job but not a lot of assets, there are no resources," says Contra Costa County family lawyer Barbara Suskind. Jennifer Gordon, head of the San Francisco Bar Association's family law section says, "If you're making $40,000, $50,000, even $60,000 a year, I don't see how you can afford a family lawyer at $200 an hour."[14] In New York, State Supreme Court Justice Emily Jane Goodman put it succinctly. "The courts are only available to the very rich, and those served by Legal Services. Legal Services only represents the smallest fraction of people, and is completely overburdened."[15]

"The biggest single problem for women in any legal service is that number one, their incomes are determined for any kind of representation — whether it is a sliding fee basis or a legal services basis or whatever — by family income," said Marcia Rochofsky of the Edhuld and Rochofsky law firm in Milwaukee, Wisconsin. "And most women, in my experience, do not have equal access to the family fund."

Rhoda Rivera, a family law attorney in Ohio, agrees. "The largest problem that women face when trying to get legal assistance is money," she said. Often lack of funds can prevent women from obtaining important legal help. A 44-year-old woman involved in a divorce case said she "couldn't afford a lawyer's fee to fight for custody of her children." Another woman added: "I work but don't make enough to afford a lawyer — yet I don't qualify for [federal] legal aid."

Even women who do have access to the family's money often have to consult their husbands about large expenditures. Such a relationship, of course, could be particularly sticky if the expenditure is to consult a lawyer. Whether by limiting her access to bank accounts or insisting that she get permission before spending large sums, husbands can, and do, financially restrict their non-working wives.

In some cases, a husband will convince his wife that to save money they should both use the same attorney in a divorce case. This is a mistake. While it is not considered unethical for the lawyer to represent both spouses, so long as he or she informs each of them of the conflict, the lawyer simply can not be the champion of both parties. Consider such an arrangement only if you have been married for a short period of time, there are no children, each party has about the same income, and there are few assets to divide. In that case, however, a do-it-yourself divorce might serve as well.[16]

Nearly 20 years ago, Congress recognized that justice without representation is impossible under the U.S. legal system, and established the Legal Services Corporation (LSC) to assist those who could not afford lawyers. Given the major decreases in funding through the 1980s, the 300 local offices affiliated with the LSC can scarcely begin to meet the demand. Pat Bath, Director of Public Information at the Legal Aid Society in New York, said that battered women and tenant evictions are given priority over divorce services, and waiting lists for help with divorces are long. Only people who are poor under the current government definitions — $11,100 a year income for a two-person family, for example — are eligible for help.[17]

The American Bar Association's Model Rules of Professional Conduct recognize that lawyers have a responsibility to provide legal services without fee, but do not mention family law as an area to be covered.[18] The problem of how to pay for the cost of divorce remains one which "urgently needs the attention of judges, legislatures and activists," concluded OWL.[19]

The New York City Department of Consumer Affairs report urges that the focus of reform should not be to figure out how to pay $50,000 attorneys' fees, but to find a better, less costly way to handle divorces. It suggests establishment of a Blue Ribbon panel to find non-adversary approaches to divorce which would preserve the assets of a marriage for the divorcing spouses, rather than handing them over to the lawyers.

With most legislatures dominated by lawyers, it seems unlikely that such a new system, which would cut the incomes of many lawyers, will be available soon.

Bias In The Courtroom

Money is the first impediment facing women seeking legal help; the second is obtaining fair and effective treatment by the individuals who run our justice system. The legal field, like other professions, is dominated by men, and still permeated by attitudes of bias against women.

A year after her testimony during confirmation hearings for Supreme Court Justice Clarence Thomas, Anita Hill told a group of women judges that stereotypes of women pervade the U.S. Court system and often block justice for victims of sexual harassment, domestic violence and date rape. "If necessary, we've got to bring some of your colleagues into the twenty-first century kicking and screaming," Hill told the group.[20]

The legal profession is still examining its collective conscience over its treatment of women. The notion that it is unethical for attorneys to have sex with their clients is still being debated, for example. John M. O'Connell called sex with clients the legal profession's "dirty little secret," in a 1992 article in the *Columbia Law Review*. "Clients," he found it necessary to point out, "may enter the legal representation vulnerable both emotionally and economically..."[21] Unfortunately, bar associations do little to discipline attorneys who sexually exploit their clients.

Studies of women's experience in the court system in several states, including New York, New Jersey, Connecticut and Rhode Island, have concluded that gender bias is widespread and of serious consequence to women. Connecticut's study, which questioned judges about their attitudes, found that women would be at a distinct disadvantage in some of the state's court rooms. One judge, for example, said he does not award alimony because it would result in women not remarrying, and he felt they should remarry. Another could not understand why a woman with a business in her home needed money for child care. As a group, the study found that judges treated women who had extra-marital affairs much more harshly than men who had done the same.[22] More than one-third of the judges thought it was not unrealistic to expect women who had been homemakers for a decade or more to be economically self-sufficient within two years of divorce.[23]

Women still make up less than 20 percent of lawyers and judges, but this is changing. Nearly 40 percent of law school graduates in 1989 were female, so women will, in time, be better represented in the courts.[24]

For now, the growing number of women and studies of gender bias have contributed to "a focus on the problem and a new sensitivity," according to Eileen McGann, a Connecticut attorney. "I was in a court room recently where the Judge kept ending each segment of the proceedings with, 'Thank you, Gentlemen,' and then would apologize each time saying, 'I'm really trying to change that.'"

Child Custody

It used to be that mothers could virtually count on being able to keep their children after a divorce. This is still true, except when husbands decide to contest custody. Then, fathers win either primary or joint physical custody most of the time — 70 percent of the time, according to a 1989 Massachusetts study.[25] Women may lose because they make less money or hold outside jobs. Following a general rule of fulfilling the "best interests of the children," more and more judges are employing economic criteria in their decisions, awarding custody of children to the parent with the greater economic resources. Usually that is the father. "It was formerly assumed that if one parent could provide a better material environment for the child, he or she could do so in the form of child support payments to the custodial parent," says Laurie Woods, Vicki Been and Joanne Schulman, of the National Center for Women & Family Law.[26] "However several states have now expressly listed this as a factor the judge must consider in determining custody. In other states, judges are considering economic factors in deciding custody even when not specifically authorized to do so by statute."

Sometimes a woman's lifestyle works against her. The mother's fitness is tested against the "traditional" mother standard, while the father's fitness is tested against the "traditional" father standard, according to the NCWFL lawyers. That puts divorced and separated mothers in a Catch-22 situation, by penalizing them for working outside the home, as well as for a lack of economic resources. "Consequently," they say, "if a woman places 'undue' emphasis upon her career — a choice she is ironically under pressure to make in order to support her child and prevent loss of custody to the father with his high income — she nevertheless stands in jeopardy of losing custody of her child."[27]

The double standard holds true when weighing the moral behavior of each parent. "It is permissible for fathers to have non-marital sexual relationships without jeopardizing custody rights," said the lawyers. "However, if a woman does so, she may well lose custody." In one court case, both parents were having new sexual relationships. Fearful of jeopardizing custody of her children — the case was still in court — the woman stopped spending the night with her new fiance. The father lived and slept with his woman friend, in a one-room hotel room with the children present. He won custody.[28]

The Massachusetts study also found a trend by judges to award shared legal custody even when parents are unable to agree on child rearing methods, or there is a history of spouse abuse.[29] So-called "friendly parent" laws in some states also now encourage joint custody. This may be particularly dangerous for a woman who has been battered, because spouse abuse is often not considered relevant in deciding child custody. The parent opposing joint custody must prove that it would actually be harmful to the child.[30]

The Woody Allen-Mia Farrow battle over custody of their children has spotlighted another aspect of custody battles: the risk of losing custody that a woman faces if she charges the father with sexually abusing the child. Writing for *The Village Voice* newspaper, Sheila Weller told a harrowing tale of a mother who lost custody after she was unsuccessful in conclusively proving sex abuse. She cited the example of Amy Neustein, a Brooklyn woman who has been denied access to her daughter since 1989 when, according to Weller, "she used a visitation to rush the girl (who was in her father's custody) to an emergency room for what the receiving doctor testified was life-saving treatment for anorexia nervosa."[31] Neustein lost custody after a judge decided she was more interested "in the fight itself" to prove abuse "than in the return of her child."[32]

Here again, the "friendly parent" laws work against the parent who raises concern about the fitness of the other parent. If the court finds those concerns lack a demonstrable basis, the "unfriendly" parent can lose custody completely.[33] It appears that judges are more prepared to believe men than women. The Massachusetts study found that a majority of probate judges believed that "mothers allege child sexual abuse to gain a bargaining advantage in the divorce process."[34] A new organization called The National Center for Protective Parents in Civil Child Sexual Abuse Cases, based in Trenton, New Jersey, has been set up to help parents who are concerned about the fitness of their divorcing spouses. H. Joan Pennington, director of the center, says that child protective services are so overwhelmed that they refuse to recognize or investigate all but the most obvious cases. Focusing on the custody issue, rather than the charges of abuse, she says, "Women and children are generally not believed by those in the legal system."[35]

Child Support

After years of determined effort, law enforcement officials, armed with new federal and state laws, have finally begun to get tough with fathers who refuse to pay child support. The reason for the action may have as much to do with the realization that child support enforcement could lower the welfare rolls, as with sympathy for the women and children involved.

"Financial deprivation due to non-support from a living parent is the primary cause of welfare dependency in the United States," concluded the U.S. Department of Health & Human Services in its 1990 report to Congress on child support enforcement.[36]

The states now have until 1994 to automatically withhold child support payments from husband's salaries. A 1992 federal law imposes for the first time criminal penalties on spouses who flee to another state to avoid paying. And many states are taking unprecedented actions to collect, ranging from posting "Wanted" posters in stores and offices (Massachusetts) to seizing cars, motorcycles or boats from unemployed or self-employed fathers (Washington), to denying or revoking the drivers' licenses of delinquent parents (California, Vermont and Arizona). The results are promising: in 1990, states collected $6 billion in child support, an 85 percent jump since 1986.[37]

It's been a long time coming. A 17-year-old boy tells of how his mother, determined to get off welfare, took two and then three jobs. "The divorce caused us not only to lose our father who did not support us, but we also lost our mom because she had to work so many jobs."[38]

Hard as they work, 32 percent of women with children whose fathers are absent lived below the official poverty level in 1989. Of the women who were supposed to get support payments that year, only half received the proper amount. Of the others, about half got nothing at all. The average amount received was a little under $3,000, so that the women still had to rely on welfare, food stamps, and other government assistance.[39]

While one might expect that the trend toward joint custody would result in more faithful and generous support, this does not appear to be the case. Awards under joint custody are "much lower," according to the National Center on Women and Family Law, and are no more likely to be paid.[40] Despite the changes in law, it is still a dismal picture.

Battered Women

More than a century ago, U.S. courts condoned wife-beating. In 1824 the Mississippi Supreme Court concluded that a "husband should be permitted to chastise his wife moderately in cases of great emergency without subjecting himself to vexatious prosecution for assault and battery, resulting in the discredit and shame of all parties concerned.' "[41] According to *The Law of Torts* by William Prosser:

> A husband or father, as the head of the household, was recognized by the early law as having authority to discipline the members of his family. He might administer to his wife "moderate correction," and "restrain" her by "domestic chastisement," although there is probably no truth whatever in the legend that he was permitted to beat her with a stick no thicker than his thumb.[42]

The law has improved, but the criminal justice system too often fails to vigorously enforce the law, and to take the threat of violence to women seriously. On New Year's Eve, 1992, Loretta McLaughlin, the *Boston Globe's* editorial page editor, chose to lead the page with an editorial titled: "Year of the Woman: In Memoriam." It began:

> In political circles, 1992 was the Year of the Woman, but for the women who have been victims of assaults by husbands and boyfriends it was a year of tragedy beyond any other. The *Globe* today prints the names of the 26 women and 18 children and bystanders who have lost their lives in Massachusetts in 1992 as a result of domestic violence. We print the list in their memory and as a call to our society and its officials that this record must not be repeated.

The litany followed. "Suzanne Beckner Hoeg, 27, stabbed and beaten with a rolling pin in front of her three children, allegedly by her estranged husband. A restraining order had expired shortly before the killing, and an arrest warrant had been issued for a previous violation."

And, "Kimberly Watkins, 10, shot by her mother's boyfriend. Her mother, Pamela, and a 14-year-old friend were shot but survived. An emergency restraining order had been issued that evening." The list went on.

In many of the cases, the women involved had obtained court orders in an attempt to protect themselves that proved futile. The Congressional Caucus for Women's Issues asserted in October 1992, that the laws concerning domestic violence are "too lenient," and "arrest is the least frequently used response" to domestic violence. It said that two-thirds of reported domestic violence incidents were classified as misdemeanors, even though half of them resulted in injuries as serious, or more serious than those resulting from rapes, robberies and aggravated assaults.[43]

As the *Boston Globe* editorial points out, domestic violence is epidemic in America. Statewide, a woman was killed by her husband or boyfriend every 14 days in 1992.

Clearly, the laws need to be strengthened and police action against batterers must be swifter and more forceful. In addition, even though experts agree that evidence of spouse abuse is one of the leading indicators of child abuse, only 10 states and the District of Columbia have laws requiring that such evidence dictate that custody of the child go only to the non-abusive parent.[44] "Custody attorneys are all too familiar with the 'but did he ever hit the children?' judicial response to wife-beating," said Joanne Schulman of the National Center for Women and Family Law.[45]

However, studies by sociologists come to a chilling conclusion: law enforcement efforts, alone, may be unable to halt spouse abuse. Several studies have found that unless a man has roots and a job in his community arrest may not stop him at all.[46] The underlying culture in America glorifies weapons and brutality and sanctions violence against women. Intensified law enforcement, educational programs for children and training for women about spousal abuse are all part of the solution to this pervasive and deplorable problem.

Taking Charge

The average marriage in United States lasts seven years.[47] Women need to take steps to protect themselves before marriage and ensure that an unanticipated divorce will not impoverish them.

■ If you are about to get married, draw up a pre-nuptial contract making clear your expectations. Equal division of the tangible and intangible assets is your goal. An agreement could prevent spending thousands extra on a divorce, if it should come to that.

■ Make sure you know your husband's Social Security number; where all the deeds and titles to major property are kept; the numbers of all your bank accounts; and the whereabouts of stock or bond certificates. In short, be fully informed about all your finances.

■ Maintain your own checking or savings account — at the very least for emergencies.

■ Familiarize yourself with the marriage laws in your state (i.e. do you live in a common law or community property state).

If you need to separate from your husband, keep these issues in mind when proceeding with legal action:

■ If your marriage has been brief, there are no children, your incomes are about equal, and there are few assets, consider a do-it-yourself divorce. Your local bookstore should have books on the subject.

■ If you gave up a career to stay home and raise the children, or took a low-paying job so your husband could go to school and prepare himself for a high-paying career, remember to focus your attention not only on the assets of your marriage, but your right to on-going support. You deserve to be compensated for your economic sacrifice.

■ As part of your divorce settlement, try to negotiate college support costs for your children. Most states do not require spouses to continue child support past age 18, and women often find themselves without any help in trying to send their children to college.

■ Don't use a lawyer who is a family friend, or who has been the family lawyer.

■ Don't choose a woman lawyer just because she is female.

■ Interview at least three attorneys before you hire one.

■ Ask your lawyer to sign a "fee arbitration agreement." In case you end up in a dispute with your lawyer about his or her fee, this agreement will provide for an arbitration process, instead of a costly lawsuit to settle the matter.

■ Get names of lawyers from people at your local women's group or church. Women who have gone through a divorce, landlord dispute or other legal actions are the best source for other women in search of a good attorney.

■ As Frances Leonard says in *Women & Money*, "Beg or borrow a lump sum to be used for a retainer up front." She points out that investing in your divorce settlement will be more important to you, in the long run, than a new car or other major purchase.

■ Know your rights when dealing with a lawyer. For example, you have the right to documents you gave your attorney. And, you have the right to know periodically how much the case is costing. See the Appendix for a copy of a suggested Bill of Rights for Divorce

Clients drafted by the New York City Department of Consumer Affairs.

■ If you believe you have been abused by your lawyer, complain to your local bar association and consumer affairs department, if you have one. If you have kept good records of your legal case, you will have a better chance of prevailing.

Do You Need An Attorney?

■ For some legal problems you may want to use a professional mediator instead of a lawyer.

■ Small Claims Court is a good avenue in which to try to collect small amounts of damages (generally under $1,000, but check your local small claims court for its requirements) and you do not need a lawyer. In fact small claims courts were first started to minimize the need for attorneys. Only a small fee is required for filing. You can call your local court for information, or stop by and ask for a pamphlet of instructions on how to file your case.

■ If you have very limited income, you may qualify for help from one of the local projects funded by the Legal Services Corporation. For example, you are eligible for legal help if your income is no more than $14,463 for a family of three. To find a local office, call the Corporation at (202) 336-8800.

Dealing With A Lawyer

■ Be open and honest. Don't hold back information. If your attorney is surprised by information you failed to disclose, your interests may be harmed.

■ Ask questions about your case and force your lawyer to explain the issues in terms you can understand. You have a right to know everything about your case, including your lawyer's strategy and time frame.

■ Don't rely on your attorney for emotional support. Your attorney should, of course, be responsive to your needs; but he or she is not a relative, marriage counselor, a psychiatrist or anything but a lawyer. Having an intimate relationship with your attorney is a bad idea. Avoid it, and fire anyone who makes improper advances.

■ Keep in touch with your lawyer, offer to help gather necessary information, and keep your attorney updated on new developments.

■ Keep track of your attorney's progress. Failure to return phone calls or letters and refusing to spend time with you may be a sign that your attorney is not putting sufficient time and effort into your case. Confront your lawyer if you think he or she is neglecting your case. If it is serious enough, you should tell the lawyer that if the neglect continues, you will see another lawyer.

■ Know your lawyer's fee structure, and ask for estimates of the total cost of your case, at various points in the process. Ask if you will receive an itemized bill each month, and whether it will show you how much time was spent on research, drafting, court and travel time. Ask if it will show who actually did the work on your case — the lawyer who you are interviewing, or an associate. Find out how much each costs per hour. Some common types of fees are:

> *Retainer fee*: This is the money that an attorney wants up front as a guarantee that in case you suddenly change your mind about needing legal help you won't leave a hardworking lawyer out in the cold. Once you have paid this fee, you have "retained" your attorney. It is credited toward the final bill, like a deposit.

Flat fee: You and your attorney may agree to a flat fee: say $500 to incorporate your business or $10,000 for your divorce. That will not change, even if your case is contested.

Range fee: The attorney may leave the final fee open — not knowing how difficult your case will be, or whether it will be contested — and instead give you a range. (It may cost between $750 and $1,000.)

Hourly fee: An hourly fee is often charged for divorce cases, and can be abused. Watch out for lawyers who have a "minimum billing unit" — the shortest time unit a lawyer bills to your file — of fifteen minutes or more. Wesley J. Smith, author of *The Lawyer's Book*, says some lawyers use this tactic to bill a 36-hour day.

Contingent fee: Your lawyer may agree that he or she will not charge you anything unless he or she wins the case, in which case he or she will take a percentage of what you win. This is a contingent fee.

Percentage fee: Percentage fees are often used in probate cases, when administering a deceased individual's estate, where the attorney takes a percentage of the estate.

You can save money by shopping around; you may find an attorney who charges less than the first one you contacted but is equally qualified. You can also try to negotiate a lower fee, by indicating that you are looking elsewhere. The important thing to keep in mind, however, is not to hire a lawyer of questionable qualifications just to save money. You may lose more in the end.

■ Know who is actually handling your case. Many law firms have paralegals, law students or younger lawyer-associates working on cases, so your attorney may not actually be personally involved in much of the case. Find out if this is the situation and exactly what aspect of your case is being handled by someone else. "Be sure you make it clear to your attorney that any work done on your case by a law student or paralegal must be work that is suitable for such a person and that their work must be closely supervised and checked by your attorney," says Joseph C. McGuinn in his book, *Lawyers: A Clients Manual.*

■ Keep a file, notepad and pocket calendar so that you write down lawyer's instructions (e.g. getting hold of a particular paper), mark them on your calendar, and carry them out on time. With a file you can keep yourself organized and maintain a record of your costs.

Getting Ready

Equip yourself with information before proceeding. Even if you are not a lawyer, you can familiarize yourself with concepts, terms and the particular laws in your state. Once you do that, the process will lose some of its mystery. You won't be intimidated and you will be more likely to get fair representation. You can go even further than that and learn to do your own legal research. Frances Leonard is the instructor in a legal research correspondence course designed for individuals with access to a law library. For more information, write to the Correspondence Division, University of California Extension, Berkeley, CA 94720, and ask about "Researching the Law."

Other Resources

Divorce and Money by Violet Woodhouse (NOLO Press, 950 Parker Street, Berkeley, CA 94710, 1992, $19.95).

Divorce and Older Women (a report published by the Older Women's League, 666 11th Street, N.W., Suite 700, Washington, D.C. 20001, 1988, $7).

The Divorce Workbook by Sally Ives, D. Fassler & M. Lash (Waterfront Books, 85 Crescent Rd, Burlington, VT, 05401, 1-800-639-6063, 1993, $12.95), for parents and children to use together; explains separation, divorce and remarriage.

Getting Free: A Handbook for Women in Abusive Relationships by Ginny NiCarthy (Seal Press, Seattle, WA 98121, 1986, 2nd edition, $12.95).

Avoiding Marketplace Perils

Joint Custody and Shared Parenting (2nd edition) Edited by Jay Folberg (Guilford Publications, 72 Spring St., New York, NY 10012, 1991, $20.95).

The Lawyer Book: A Nuts and Bolts Guide to Client Survival by Wesley J. Smith (Price Stern Sloan, Los Angeles, CA, 1987), This book is no longer in print but it is available in libraries).

Practical Divorce Solutions by Charles Sherman (NOLO Press, 950 Parker Street, Berkeley, CA 94710, 1990, $12.95).

The Rights of Women by Susan Ross and Ann Barcher (Southern Illinois University Press, P.O. Box 3694, Carbondale, IL 62902, 1993, $7.95).

NOLO Press, 950 Parker Street, Berkeley, CA 94710, publishes a wide variety of consumer law books.

Other Organizations with Valuable Information

Center for Women Policy Studies 2000 P Street, N.W., Suite 508, Washington, D.C. 20036. Provides information on legal assistance for battered women, information on sexual harassment and family policy issues.

Coalition for Family Justice, 821 Broadway, Irvington-On-Hudson, New York 10533. Provides information and advice on divorce and selecting an attorney, child support, and custody.

EXPOSE (Ex-Partners of Servicemen/women for Equality), P.O. Box 11191, Alexandria, VA 22312. Provides information on legal and financial concerns. Publishes *A Guide to Military Separation & Divorce* for $5.

National Center for Protective Parents, 1908 Riverside Drive, Trenton, NJ 08618. Assists parents when allegations of child sexual abuse are raised during a divorce, custody, or visitation proceeding.

National Center on Women and Family Law, 799 Broadway, Room 402, New York, NY 10003. Researches and publishes reports and other materials on topics concerning women and family law, including battered women, child custody, child support and divorce. Publishes the bi-monthly newsletter, *The Women's Advocate*.

National Coalition Against Domestic Violence, P.O. Box 1874, Denver, CO 80218-0749. A national group of grassroots shelter and service programs for battered women. Provides technical assistance and training to end personal and societal violence against women and children. Publishes *The Voice* three times a year.

NOW Legal Defense and Education Fund, 99 Hudson Street, 12th Floor, New York, NY 10013. Litigates and lobbies on policy issues concerning equality of women. Provides resource kits on divorce, child custody, battered women and other topics for $5 per kit. (Note: when ordering kit write "Attention Intake Paralegal" on envelope.)

Women's Legal Defense Fund, 1875 Connecticut Avenue, N.W., Suite 710, Washington, D.C. 20009. Lobbying, litigation and community organizing to achieve equality for women. Issues include family and medical leave, affirmative action, sexual harassment and wage discrimination. Publishes *WLDF News* twice a year.

WOW (Wider Opportunities for Women), 1325 G Street, N.W., Suite 710, Washington, D.C. 20009. Works with economically disadvantaged women to help them achieve economic independence and equality. Publishes *Women At Work* twice a year.

Chapter Five

Advertising

When a single voice badgers or degrades women in the workplace because of their gender, we call it sexual harassment. When that voice is amplified for millions of people by millions of dollars, we call it advertising.
Ronald K.L. Collins, co-founder of the Center for the Study of Commercialism.

Ever since the emergence of mass advertising encouraging people to mindlessly consume — and to keep consuming — Madison Avenue has instilled in women insecurity and anxiety about their looks, their housekeeping, their relationships, even their natural body processes. Ad makers have exploited those negative emotions by offering products that promise to relieve the very feelings of inadequacy they nurtured in the first place.

Advertising, along with rampant commercialism, respects no boundaries. Advertising has taught women to be constant self-critics, and to look critically — or enviously — at other women. It steals a woman's "love of herself as she is and offers it back to her for the price of a product," writes critic and novelist John Berger.[1]

Advertising, in old and new forms, like the music industry's commercials that fill the hours of MTV programming, fosters contempt for women by men and encourages men's fantasies of women as subservient sex objects whose only role is to gratify male needs.

Why Women Pay More

Advertising has responded to the women's liberation movement by perverting women's expressed desires for real independence and substituting, instead, the notion that these goals can be achieved through buying lotions, hair dyes, cigarettes and perfume.

The advertising industry has also failed women by not performing one of its legitimate roles: to inform women about the products and services they truly need. Only recently have car makers, for examples, realized that women buy cars and begun aiming ads at them. The number of such ads, however, is still far below those directed to men. Other makers of products that women buy — appliances, electronics, office equipment and investment funds, to name a few — still often ignore women, making it harder for women to make informed purchases.

■ What haven't we been taught about our eye lashes? "Are there limits?" asks Maybelline in an ad for — no kidding — "Illegal Lengths" mascara. "Not for some women. Or their lashes. So unlawfully long, so remarkably strong, they're almost dangerous." Who would have guessed eyelashes could be dangerous?

■ Women are constantly informed that looking very young is desirable, and that an older look, that might reveal experience, maturity or power, is to be avoided at all cost. In a neat twist of reality, Clairol tells us dyed or bleached hair is not phony. No, its ad proclaims, "gray hair lies. Gray hair says you're old, when you're not! That's why you need Miss Clairol."

■ Cigarette ads, of course, would not dare tell us — except in the small type of the required Surgeon General's warning — that smoking cigarettes can kill you. Instead, Virginia Slims shows us a lovely, healthy, young woman straddling a motor cycle: "I don't necessarily want to run the world, but I wouldn't mind taking it for a little ride," says this image of the liberated woman.

■ The now infamous "Swedish Bikini Team" consisted of five blonde women who descended from the sky for the amusement of a grinning group of men. "It Does Not Get Better," proclaims this ad that the Stroh Brewing Co.

Advertising, of course, is only one element of the larger culture that creates these stereotypes. Some advertisers have improved their ads, motivated by a new sensitivity to women and the fact that it makes good business sense. But advertising, as media critic and scholar Dr. Jean Kilbourne said in an interview, "reflects only what's going to be good for business." It perpetuates stereotypes if they encourage women to buy, and some of the most damaging stereotypes are used to push vastly over-priced-products and services that women may not need in the first place.

Years ago, people spoke of the military industrial complex that worked to perpetuate America's war machine. Today, an unholy alliance of some advertisers, captive magazines and other media is helping to perpetuate women's inequality in the marketplace.

A Woman's Place

Since the industrial revolution, women have been trained as the purchasing agents and managers of their households. "While women were cultivated as general purchasing managers for the household, the basic definition of men in the ads was as bread-winners, wage earners," writes Stuart Ewen, author of *Captains of Consciousness*.[2]

During the early part of the twentieth century, advertisers offered housewives thousands of new products and machines that promised to free them from household drudgery — vacuum cleaners, toasters, electric blenders, can openers, washing machines. But housework remained a full-time job, as women were exhorted to pay attention to minute household details. At the end of the day she would still be exhausted.

Why Women Pay More

Advertising through the 1970s defined the successful housewife as one who had to have polished floors and furniture, bright and sweet-smelling laundry and shining silver. As a 1977 study by the Canadian Advertising Advisory Board explained, "it is the cumulative impact of a whole series of commercials showing household products in use, with women demonstrating the products — often with enthusiasm bordering on ecstasy... [that viewers] find incredible, hilarious or insulting."

For a while, in the 1980s, advertisers designed ads for Superwoman — the female business executive who could "bring home the bacon" as well as fry it up for dinner. They also began to take note of men's changing roles. Researcher Lynn T. Lovdal found that in television commercials, men were "three times as likely in 1988 as in 1978 to pitch domestic products like spaghetti sauce or fabric softener," according to a report in *American Demographics*.[3]

However, commercial authority figures are still most often men. In more than eight out of 10 commercials, the "voiceover," or narrator, who delivers the "buy this" message, is male.[4] The reason? "Tradition," explains Stanley R. Becker, vice chairman of Saatchi & Saatchi, a major ad firm. To his credit, he goes on to say that perhaps he should re-examine this knee-jerk casting.[5]

In the 1990s, advertisers and manufacturers have begun to realize that most women are out working, in addition to running their homes. Women have realized it is not humanly possible for anyone to do it "all," if "all" means meals cooked from scratch; mirror-like floors and a spotless house; quality time with the children; a job; a happy husband and a "great figure." Some day men may become equal partners in domestic chores, but that day has not yet arrived. A recent market research study conducted for *American Demographics* found that only 12 percent of married men do all the food shopping for their households, whereas two-thirds of women do all or most of the spending for their family's household items.[6]

What women need now are products and services that truly save time. The effectiveness of guilt-based advertising of household products has waned. Women are more responsive to ads that stress value for the dollar, convenience, efficiency and service.

To Be Young, Thin and Beautiful

One demand, however, has remained relentless, and in fact, intensified: the desire to look young, thin, and beautiful according to current "beauty" standards. Reinforced by television, movies and magazines that almost exclusively show only such women, ads promise that most women can achieve the desired image if only they will spend enough money. Unfortunately, women spend billions yearly on diet programs, diet foods and cosmetics.

An astonishing half of all women in this country may be on a diet at any moment in time.[7] But almost all are doomed to failure. Study after study has shown that regardless of method, staying permanently at a lower weight after a diet is a goal achieved by very few.

For example, Thomas Wadden, an obesity expert at Syracuse University, studied 517 people who were at least 30 percent overweight according to current government weight tables. Each enrolled in a 26-week program that started with a very low-calorie liquid formula diet, and then increased food intake to 1,500 calories a day. They also took classes to help them modify their lifestyle. Results: only 285 people finished the program; these people lost an average of 53 pounds. After a year, only 67 of the original 517 people had maintained a weight loss of 22 pounds or more.[8]

Advertising, however, paints a very different picture:

■ "You can call the Optifast program today and have all you need to control your weight for the rest of your life," says an ad for Optifast.

■ "...[Y]ou will not experience a rebound phenomenon (regain lost weight) after you attain your goal," says an ad for Medifast.

■ "Weight Loss Myth #4: Once You Lose It, You'll Gain it Back... with the support of the ULTRAFAST Program, you get a new attitude. The weight stays off," says an ad for Ultrafast.

The manufacturers of these liquid diets were all the subject of Federal Trade Commission (FTC) complaints of deceptive and unsubstantiated claims. The manufacturers of all three products agreed to settlements promising they would no longer make such claims unless they disclosed the average weight loss of their clients and the length of time they maintained the loss. However, the FTC did nothing to reimburse clients who had spent from $1,400 to $2,800 for the programs because they believed the false claims.[9]

In its pamphlet, *The Facts About Weight Loss*, the FTC warns consumers about a number of other phony pills, devices and gadgets that all promise help with weight loss. The list includes: fat blockers, starch blockers, diet patches, electric muscle stimulators and weight loss "earrings" that purport to stimulate acupuncture points. In short, none of them work.

Many overweight people, of course, should lose weight, particularly those with family histories of diabetes, heart disease or high blood pressure. False advertising, however, does nothing to help you lose anything but money. The wisdom of the most objective experts points to the need for a low-fat, high-carbohydrate diet and regular exercise as the only long-term "cure" for obesity.

Some help, in this regard, has just come from the federal government which has now defined the meaning of terms like "light" and "low-fat" used in food labelling. "Light," for example, may be used only if the food has 50 percent less fat than the food to which it is being compared. By May 1994, all food labels will also have to reveal how much of their caloric content comes from fat, along with other useful nutrition information.[10] This action by the Food and Drug Administration (FDA) came 11 years after it first proposed such regulations, and only after the Congress passed the Nutrition Labelling and Education Act in 1990.

Cosmetic ads are even less based in reality than ads for weight loss products, and are much less subject to regulation. As long as advertisers don't make medical claims for their products, they can say just about anything — and they do. In fact, the FDA cannot even require that cosmetics be safety tested before being put on the market. In 1989, the FDA identified 130 chemicals used in cosmetics that it recommended be safety-tested, and then took no further action.[11]

Cosmetic ads speak mysteriously of "liposomes" and "nayad" and "cerebrosides" and promise wonders from human placenta and vitamins that you can absorb through the skin simply by shampooing your hair. Do these ingredients do more than just swell the price of the products? The manufacturers claim they do, but don't have to prove it.

The best proof available, perhaps, is the testing done by Consumers Union, whose magazine, *Consumer Reports*, accepts no advertising. In February 1989, Consumers Union tested shampoos, for example, on 49 women volunteers. The shampoos were rated on sudsing, ease of rinsing, ease of combing and shininess of the hair when dry. The result: the top-rated shampoo was the relatively inexpensive Pert Plus, which cost less than half as much as many other shampoos which received poorer ratings. "Disappointing though it may be," said Consumers Union, "no tested shampoo made hair shinier than any other."[12]

Consumers Union also tested facial cleansers, giving a panel of women unmarked jars of the products to try over a period of 10 weeks.

The women ended up rating Olay Beauty Cleanser, then priced at 85 cents an ounce, as highly as Elizabeth Arden Skin Wash, costing $2.13 an ounce.[13]

Clearly, women need to raise their consciousness and understand that the goal of these sophisticated ad techniques is to sell products.

The Unholy Alliance

One of the reasons women are not skeptical of cosmetic advertising is that women's magazines constantly praise the latest skin creams and make-up in articles on beauty and health. According to Gloria Steinem, many women are surprised to learn that these articles are demanded by advertisers.

Steinem, one of the founders of *Ms.* magazine, said in an interview that during her frequent lectures to community groups, women are clearly startled to learn "that it's never been any other way for women's magazines. Women's magazines started out as catalogs into which they slipped a few articles." The editors and writers for these magazines, to their credit, try hard to sandwich in meaningful articles among the ads. However, they are so dependent on the money paid them by cosmetic advertisers that they must constantly run articles on beauty make-overs, new hair styles, diets and diet products, to name a few staples. They are vulnerable to this economic blackmail because advertisers of other kinds of products — from cars to computers to insurance — don't find women's magazines a suitable environment for their messages. It's a vicious circle.

Naomi Wolf, author of *The Beauty Myth*, calls advertisers "the West's courteous censors."[14] As Gloria Steinem wrote in the first issue of *Ms.* magazine published without advertising, it isn't just cosmetic advertisers who dictate editorial content in women's magazines:

Food advertisers have always demanded that women's magazines publish recipes and articles on entertaining (preferably ones that name their products) in return for their ads; clothing advertisers expect to be surrounded by fashion spreads (especially ones that credit their designers); and shampoo, fragrance and beauty products in general usually insist on positive editorial coverage of beauty subjects, plus photo credits besides.[15]

Add to her list tobacco companies, that ask for something else from women's magazines: silence on the risks of smoking. Helen Gurley Brown, editor of *Cosmopolitan*, has already candidly observed that she was not about to bite the hand that fed her.

The more cigarette ads a magazine carries, the less likely it will be to carry articles on the dangers of smoking, according to the findings of a 1992 study titled, "Cigarette Advertising and Magazine Coverage," in which researchers conducted a statistical analysis of 99 U.S. magazines published over a 25-year period.[16] "This relation was particularly strong in the case of women's magazines," said the study's authors.[17]

The tobacco companies threaten to pull more than their cigarette ads. Today's tobacco companies are conglomerates with many product lines. So when the ad agency Saatchi & Saatchi prepared ads featuring the no-smoking policy of client Northwest Airlines, RJR/Nabisco cancelled its $80 million contract with Saatchi for food ads.[18]

It used to be that far more men smoked than women. In 1965, one out of two men over 18 years smoked, but only about one in three women did. Today, only a slightly higher percentage of men than women smoke, although the number for both men and women is now about one in four.[19] Some studies report that women have more withdrawal symptoms when they try to quit, and that women are far more concerned with the weight gain often associated with quitting than men.[20]

That women now smoke as much as men is no accident: the tobacco industry has targeted cigarette ads at women for a long time, linking themes of independence, liberation and slenderness to special brands, like Virginia Slims.

For the most part, women's magazines are still shunned by all but the sellers of fashions, food, cosmetics and tobacco. A casual review of late 1992 magazines shows Chrysler, Nissan and Saturn starting to place a limited number of ads in women's magazines. Toyota even placed an ad for one of its pick-up trucks in the December 1992 issue of *Glamour*. But take a look at magazines targeted to men, such as *Esquire* and *Gentlemen's Quarterly*, and the contrast is immediately clear. These magazines have ads for a wide variety of products like travel destinations, binoculars, cellular telephones, investment funds, software, alcoholic beverages (a big category for men), and, of course, cars.

Sex Sells

While advertisers may have stopped, out of necessity, using guilt to sell us floor wax, they have not stopped using sex to sell just about everything. Younger people no longer remember the airline ad that showed an attractive young stewardess saying, "Fly me, I'm Barbara," which infuriated so many women. But today, sexist images are "more blatant than ever before," according to Dr. Kilbourne. She writes:

> The sex object is a mannequin, a shell. She has no lines or wrinkles, no scars or blemishes; indeed she has no pores. She is thin, tall and long-legged, and above all young... A woman is conditioned to view her face as a mask and her body as an object.[21]

Designer Calvin Klein is notorious for creating advertising that uses women and sexual images to sell products. In the early 1980s, actress Brooke Shields purred, "Nothing comes between me and my Calvins." A few years later, ads for Eternity fragrance featured a woman saying, "Help me, destroy me, become me, until there's nothing left of me, nothing left but you."[22]

Avoiding Marketplace Perils

Other advertisers are even more blatant in their exploitation of women's bodies. Valerie Salembier, publisher of *Family Circle* magazine, described a print ad for Diesel jeans as "unbearable in its insensitivity to both women and minorities." The ad is set against a zebra print showing an African American women wearing only a bra and jeans with the fly undone. The caption reads, "How to control wild animals."[23]

A late 1992 magazine ad for Guess Jeans shows a Marilyn Monroe look-alike with a zip-front dress that's hanging off one shoulder as if someone has either just started removing it or she hasn't quite finished putting it back on. Maybe the timing clue is the cigarette she's smoking.

The music video cable station, MTV, meanwhile, uses sex to sell tapes and CDs and other products all day long as its music videos are presented to impressionable adolescents as entertainment, instead of what they are — a sophisticated form of selling. Professor Sut Jhally, a media critic at the University of Massachusetts at Amherst, examined images from more than 150 rock videos. He describes the use of sexual images to sell music products this way:

> One of the things I focused on was how the camera consumes women's bodies, moves up and down, etc. But even those are fairly brief shots, and their purpose basically is to keep you watching. If they made the whole video like that, you would watch in a different way. That's what advertising does so well. The sex is fragmentary, the sex is there in concentrated bursts, and you look at it, and it hits you, and it's gone. It's a strategy to make you watch harder, to make sure that they've got your attention...[24]

Jhally has made his own video highlighting sexist images on MTV, which includes such scenes as Rod Stewart's face framed by anonymous female legs as he appears to jam his microphone up between them, and David Lee Roth's use of mannequin-like women. At the end of his video, he superimposes statistics on rape over an MTV scene showing a young woman crawling toward the camera on her hands and knees. His point, he says, is not that he believes MTV causes violence against women, but that it contributes to an environment that does.[25]

But the sexist ad that may have the most permanent place in history came to us from the Stroh Brewery Company. Stroh's Swedish Bikini Team ad moved eight female workers at its St. Paul, Minnesota brewery to file a sexual harassment lawsuit against Stroh. The women charged that they were fondled, insulted by crude remarks and surrounded by sexist magazines and fliers at the plant. They claim that the ads encouraged their tormentors. Stroh denied the harassment charges, and also asserts that the ads were not sexist. Even if they were, the company notes, the ads are constitutionally protected free speech, a point supported by some civil liberties lawyers.[26] The suit is still pending.

The Fund for the Feminist Majority urged women to send letters of protest to Stroh, noting in a report that *Playboy* magazine described the Bikini Team ad as "five buxom blondes designed to make men sweatier than the coldest bottle of brew." Such ads, said the Fund, "are a typical example of how our male-dominated society interweaves sexism and racism in the most insidious ways."

Ronald K.L. Collins, co-founder of the Center for the Study of Commercialism, noted that, "The law tells the men at Stroh not to treat women as sex objects, while company ads tell them to revel in the thought. The five women of St. Paul have turned to the courts to reaffirm a single message — sexual oppression in all of its forms is an affront to civilized society."[27]

The Power of Suggestion

Suggestive and alluring images, rather than claims on the merits of the products itself, are commonly used in selling to women. John Berger writes that advertising "proposes to each one of us that we transform ourselves and our lives by buying something more... [It] persuades us of such transformation by showing us people who have apparently been transformed and are, as a result, enviable... [Ads] are about social relations, not objects; promises not of pleasure but of happiness."[28]

That is especially true for advertising aimed at women. Through images, advertisers promise women a new life if they buy their products: "Suzanne Stehlik bought a Saturn coupe because she didn't have enough excitement in her life," says one of the newer — and still relatively uncommon — car ads aimed at women. Stehlik is pictured indulging in her favorite sport, sky-diving. The excitement theme consumes the entire magazine ad, leaving no room for a discussion of horsepower or transmission or anti-lock brakes — items of information that are standard in traditional male-oriented car ads.

Perfume ads are a good example of how images are used to sell the product: they boldly create images of romantic fantasy worlds — riding on a white horse bareback through a field of flowers, warm autumn nights in France, tropical islands in the sun, a handsome young man gazing tenderly down on a woman lying in bed.

Unfortunately, ads affect some women, subtly but powerfully, because we are taught these ways of seeing ourselves. Unable to measure up to the "beautiful women" or the "happy housewives" in the ads we see, some women experience feelings of inadequacy. "It makes us feel incredibly insecure," says Kilbourne.

For some women consumers, the messages sent by advertising can be debilitating. Bombarded by hundreds of these messages each day — that women are nice to look at but should not be taken seriously — merchants and manufacturers, doctors and lawyers continue to treat women according to old-fashioned stereotypes: the message is not only that such treatment is OK but that women expect it. Thus, you may find yourself the butt of jokes by an auto mechanic, your body sized up by a male loan officer, your questions ignored by your doctor.

"As a consumer what you most want is to be taken seriously," says Kilbourne. "And that is exactly what women are not."

As a result of both advertising and the way women have been trained, they are often less assertive in situations that require a take- charge attitude, less likely to challenge an unscrupulous repairperson, less likely to ask questions of a lawyer or doctor. Many women shy away from confrontation, instead letting the people they pay for goods and services bowl them over. We slowly begin to lose control over our own lives.

Change Ahead?

Advertisers know they must always change with the times. They know that the baby boom generation of women is maturing, and that women's sensibilities have been heightened in this post-Anita Hill era. Count Calvin Klein among those who have gotten the wake-up call. In the spring of 1992, he used 40-year-old model Lisa Taylor in a series of successful ads.[29] While not a significant measure of progress, some beer companies, like Miller, have realized that women are a market for their products, and have devised ads showing female rodeo riders, jazz dancers and surfers.

Seeking to avoid a costly and embarrassing mistake, such as Stroh made with the bikini team, several New York City ad agencies and some manufacturers have asked advice from feminists before they complete ads. Some agencies, like the New York-based Bozell agency, have even held sex-in-advertising seminars for their own staffs.[30]

What is needed, however, is more fundamental and far-reaching. Since government appears reluctant to regulate advertising, much more vigorous "self-regulation" is needed. The Canadian Advertising Foundation sponsors advisory panels that include advertisers, agencies, media representatives and members of the general public. The panels are responsible for education and sensitivity programs, and handle complaints.

If an ad is found to violate a set of guidelines, the panel tries to have the ad changed or stopped.

The guidelines (See Appendix) cover not only sexuality "on display merely for the gratification of others," but also use of language, and the need to portray women and men of all ages, ethnicities, backgrounds and appearances in ads. They suggest that both men and women should be shown doing household tasks and making decisions about buying both large and small items. They also encourage the ad industry to portray women and men equally in authority roles.

Kerry Kerr, a spokesperson for the Foundation, said that advertisers "usually cooperate" and correct ads that the panels judge to have violated the guidelines. She attributed the lack of a parallel group in the United States to our attitude that we are entitled to do anything we want, whereas Canadians are somewhat more accepting of restrictions.

These days commercialism has reached its tentacles further than ever before. With ads in books, movie theaters, at sporting events, in doctors and dentists' reception rooms, and even in schools — through the controversial Channel One, — an important balance has been lost. With leaders such as Ronald K.L. Collins of the Center for the Study of Commercialism urging government action to declare at least some spheres of life commercial-free, U.S. advertisers might look north to Canada for an alternative.

Taking Charge

The first step toward getting out from under the thumb of advertisers is developing a critical eye. When you look at an ad, ask yourself some of these questions:

Are sexual stereotypes perpetuated in the ad?

Are the women portrayed as stupid, or incapable of making important decisions?

Does the ad use belittling language toward women?

Does the ad portray women as more neurotic than men?

Is there suggestive sexual language about women's role or bodies?

Is the woman shown in an alluring, suggestive position?

Does the ad portray women in a situation that tends to confirm the view that women are the property of men?

Do I really want and need this product or am I reacting to suggestive images?

Is the ad suggesting that I can look like the beautiful model in it?

Does the ad promote the idea that all women have to be slender and "young-looking?"

Does the ad show working or professional women as sex objects?

What can you do:

■ If you find an ad particularly offensive, write to the advertiser. You can say that you intend not to buy their product because of the ad. Get your friends to write letters too. If an ad on television is troubling, ask the local television station if you or a friend could respond with a guest editorial about how women are portrayed in advertising.

■ Sensitize your children to offensive advertising. Watch MTV with them and point out to them that this so-called programming is actually a stream of sophisticated advertising. Explain that women are exploited when they are used as "eye candy" to rivet the attention of watchers to the video.

■ Set an example for your children by refusing to buy over-priced cosmetics that are sold through fantasy advertising. Save money by buying less expensive products of equal quality.

■ Seek out and support objective sources of information. *Consumer Reports* takes no advertising and rates products on their important attributes, not the cleverness of their ads. *Ms.* magazine also takes no advertising and presents articles on a range of concerns to women.

■ If you are concerned about the over-commercialization of U.S. life, contact the Center for the Study of Commercialism, 1875 Connecticut Ave. N.W., Suite 300, Washington D.C. 20009, or call (202) 797-7080.

■ Set up a meeting for your community group, office, school, church group or club on advertising for women, and show Jean Kilbourne's video, "Still Killing Us Softly." It is available for rent or purchase from Cambridge Documentary Films, P.O. Box 385, Cambridge, MA 02139, or call (617) 354-3677.

Weight Loss

If you are thinking of signing up for any weight loss program, ask the following questions before you hand over your money:

> What percentage of people who start the program finish it?
>
> How many of the people who finish the program lose weight, and what is their average weight loss?
>
> How many of these people maintain a weight loss after one, three and five years? How much weight did they keep off?
>
> What percentage of participants experienced any adverse medical or psychological effects, and what were they?
> If you don't get good answers to these questions — or if the "counselor" says you are just being negative, take your business elsewhere.

Other Resources:

Backlash by Susan Faludi (Crown Publishers, New York, NY, 1991, $12.50), an examination of women's status in U.S. society, including how advertising and the media has spread a backlash against women's advancement.

The Beauty Myth, by Naomi Wolf (Bantam Doubleday, New York, NY, 1991, $11), an analysis of how advertising has promoted and manipulated women's beauty insecurities.

Being Beautiful by Ralph Nader and Katherine Isaac (Center for Study of Responsive Law, P.O. Box 19367, Washington, D.C. 20036, 1986, $10), encourages independent thinking about beauty and beauty products.

Consumer Guide to Advertising (American Association of Retired Persons, 1909 K Street, N.W., Washington, D.C. 20049, $17.50), a guide to recognizing deceptive advertising.

Avoiding Marketplace Perils

Cultural Politics in Contemporary America by I. Angus, and S. Jhally (Routledge, London, 1989, $15.95), a collection of essays by media critics on advertising and stereotypes.

Still Killing Us Softly: Advertising's Image of Women (Cambridge Documentary Films, Inc., P.O. Box 385, Cambridge, MA 02139, 1987, $46/day/rental or $425 to purchase), a 30-minute film about advertising's continuing assault on the self-images of women, men and children.

Selling America's Kids: Commercial Pressures on Kids of the 90s (Consumers Union, 101 Truman Avenue, Yonkers, NY 10703, 1990, $2).

Other Organizations with Valuable Information

Center for the Study of Commercialism, 1875 Connecticut Avenue, N.W., Suite 300, Washington, D.C. 20009. Researches and publicizes the excessive intrusion of commercial interests in society.

Center for Media and Values, 1962 South Shenandoah Street, Los Angeles, CA 90034. Publishes the magazine *Media & Values*, and *Break the Lies that Bind*, a curriculum package on sexism in the media.

Challenging Media Images of Women, P.O. Box 902, Framingham, MA 01701. A national organization challenging sexist, racist and abusive images in the media. Publishes *Challenging Media Images of Women*, a quarterly newsletter.

FAIR (Fairness & Accuracy in Reporting), 130 West 25th Street, New York, NY 10001. A national media watch group focusing on the narrow corporate ownership of the press and its biased and inadequate coverage of issues relating to women, labor and minorities. Publishes *Extra!* eight times a year.

Institute for Media Education, P.O. Box 7404 Arlington, VA 22207. Provides materials on children, pornography and violence.

Media Watch, 1803 Mission Street, Suite 7, Santa Cruz, CA 95060. Publishes *Media Watch*, a quarterly newsletter dedicated to improving the image of women in the media.

National Coalition on Television Violence, P.O. Box 2157 Champaign, IL 61825.

PTA Television Project, 700 North Rush Street, Chicago, IL 60611.

Why Women Pay More

Provides a free brochure *Children & Family & Television.*

Women Against Pornography, 321 West 47th Street, New York, NY 10036. Publishes *Write Back, Fight Back*, a guide to changing the media through letter writing.

WOW (Wider Opportunities For Women), 1325 G Street, N.W., Washington, D.C. 20005. Publishes several reports on how women are portrayed in the media, including *What's Wrong with this Picture* (covering the status of women in entertainment TV), and *Growing up in Prime Time: An Analysis of Adolescent Girls on Television.*

Chapter Six

Fashion

...inside the majority of the West's controlled, successful working women, there is a secret "underlife" poisoning our freedom; infused with notions of beauty, it is a dark vein of self-hatred, physical obsessions, terror of aging, and dread of lost control.[1]
Naomi Wolf

Since the days when Amelia Bloomer invented a pants-like alternative to the enormous skirts that kept women from active pursuits, feminists have understood how fashion has pressured women to define and describe themselves as weak and helpless ornaments, wearing clothes that hamper their activity and movements — and too often cripple them or otherwise harm their health.

We can look back now in wonder and sympathy at the Chinese women whose feet were wrapped and bound so they could not grow, so as to appeal to the warped desires of men who thought doll-size feet on grown women were sexy. We can read *Gone with the Wind* and be amazed at Scarlet's haste after child-birth to get back into her corset. We can laugh at the creations that hairdressers built atop women's heads in the eighteenth century, and then wonder how it was possible to sleep or perform the tasks we now consider ordinary, or how it felt when this construction of hair itched and pulled and begged to be torn off.

In her book, *The Beauty Myth*, Naomi Wolf makes the case that the very feminism which freed women from the traditional dictates of fashion has resulted in a backlash that has actually intensified the beauty demands placed on women. No longer must we contend just with our hemlines or the cut of our sleeves.

Why Women Pay More

Today women, are being held to the impossible standard of beauty exemplified by high fashion models. Tall and almost impossibly thin, mannequin-like images of women used to populate only fashion runways and fashion magazines. Now, they fill movie screens and television advertisements, and most all media — to the exclusion of virtually all other ages, sizes and shapes of women. (See the Advertising Chapter).

All these images affect us. Studies of female college students show that they compare themselves to models and envy them their looks. In one study, one-third of the young women questioned said that clothing and cosmetic ads made them feel dissatisfied with themselves. The problem appears to be that women — and men — no longer consider professional models as a special category of people with whom it is ridiculous to compare non-models. This so-called contrast effect caused men and women who were shown nude photos of women, who were not professional models, to rate them lower in attractiveness after they were shown centerfolds in *Playboy* and *Penthouse*.[2]

Some women are motivated by these images to emulate the models. They will diet and exercise — almost to obsession — and undergo surgical procedures and spend tens of billions of dollars on cosmetics and trips to the beauty parlor to reach this often unattainable goal.

Many of us enjoy the quest for a fit body, the artistry of make-up and the wearing of stylish clothes. That's great, so long as guilt and fear are not driving us, and we are not wasting our money and time, sacrificing our health or limiting our education or ambitions in order to conform to the current beauty standards.

Women can overcome fears about aging and of being overweight. Women can use their money intelligently to gain economic security for themselves. And women can reject fashions that are harmful or inhibiting to our development as people.

Clothes Make the Woman

What women wear affects the way they are treated in the marketplace, which includes not only their place of work but in the marketplace as consumers. Women not only need the respect of their bosses and peers or subordinates at work, but they also need to be treated with respect by service technicians, doctors, lawyers and sales clerks.

"There is no question in my mind that many women are held back in their job progress because of inattention to dress, wrote Betty Lehan Harragan in *Games Mother Never Taught You.* "If your clothes don't convey the message that you are competent, able, ambitious, self-confident, reliable and authoritative, nothing you say or do will overcome the negative signals emanating from your apparel."

This message is contrary to the conditioning women have experienced.

Many girls are taught to dress for attention, and not for respect, according to Allison Lurie, author of *The Language of Clothes.*
"Sex-typing in dress begins at birth with the assignment of pale-pink layettes, toys, bedding and furniture to girl babies and pale-blue ones to boy babies," writes Lurie. "Pink in this context is associated with sentiment, blue with service. The implication is that the little girl's future concern will be the life of the affections; the boy's earning a living."

Girls' versions of tricycles, bicycles and even Legos come in pink and lavender. Girls clothes feature flowers and domestic animals, while boy's clothes are usually made in darker colors and "printed with designs involving sports, transportation and cute wild animals. The suggestion is that the boy will play vigorously and travel over long distances; the girls will stay home and nurture plants and small mammals," wrote Lurie.

The clothes a young girl wears may strongly affect her later life. First, a girl who is overly concerned about her appearance may give up the chance to play sports or to break free of stereotypes and choose a well-paying "male" job like auto repair mechanic. She may be less assertive than other girls, and have fragile self-esteem. "The presence of a girl 'all dolled up' is unreal," said Dr. Selma Greenberg of Hofstra University, who has studied how little girls behave and how adults respond to them depending on their dress. "She is unable to move. She is sweet. She is cute. Girls become too dependent on others' opinions of them."

Second, as fashion buyers, girls are taught to rank attractiveness over utility, comfort and quality. "Very young girls get a lot of attention if they participate in the expected behaviors," said Greenberg. "Girls get a lot more praise than boys... but for the wrong reasons. The praise is for appearing decorative. Girls are praised on appearance. They are almost never praised on accomplishment. Boys are praised for activity; girls are praised for passivity."

Some women have consciously or unconsciously followed fashion. And, unfortunately some women and men still believe that achieving a comfortable, secure life-style is linked to how they look. And, that looks are linked to attracting a spouse with high earning potential.

Progress has been made, however. Fewer women these days are sacrificing comfort and mobility for style than ever before in recent history. There is one huge exception to this trend: shoes.

In Step, In Pain

The pointed toe, high-heel shoes that most women continue to buy — and the ones principally offered by manufacturers — not only hobble women but are dangerous (not unlike the ancient practice of foot binding in China). Stiletto heels, which make their wearer appear long-legged, force women to take small steps instead of on-the-ground strides.

Women have tried to send a message to manufacturers that they have jobs to do. For years now, working women have been donning sneakers and running shoes for the commute to work. No, sneakers don't match a suit, but they have been a far better choice than trying to run for the subway in high heels. Once women get to their work places, they change into their heels.

Most women will admit it: high heeled, pointed toe shoes hurt. Make them backless, open-toed or strap sandals for evening wear and they are extremely painful. Drop by any wedding party after the cake is cut and count the women dancing in their bare feet.

Indeed, years ago, when Dr. Claire Nader was doing research on shoe styles (platforms were then in vogue, as they are again now) she walked into the "better shoes department" of Garfinckels' Department Store in Washington, D.C. and asked the sales clerk if he would help her find some comfortable shoes. His response was: "What's wrong with your feet? Do you have a problem?" Clearly, he did not think that comfort was a consideration in most women's choice of shoes.

Platform shoes present women with a different set of problems than high heels. The rigid, thick platform sole, interrupts the normal reflex pattern of walking, placing abnormal strain on the ankles, legs, and hips. The danger of falling is acute. The last time platform shoes were in style in the 1970s, the press reported that a Manhattan woman fell down a flight of stairs after she tripped on her platform shoe. The woman fractured a bone in her toes, and was on crutches for six weeks. Singer Kay Starr reportedly fell off a pair of backless clogs, broke two bones in her foot, and was in and out of a cast for three months. Platform shoes were also known to cause auto accidents by preventing the driver from distinguishing the accelerator from the brake.

Podiatrists say that the majority of their patients are women. Since men and women are born with similar feet, common sense suggests — and the podiatrists tell us — that the major reason so many women have foot problems is the shoes they wear. Among the reasons women go to podiatrists are bunions. Bunions, said Dr. Harold B. Glickman, a Washington, D.C. podiatrist, are a malalignment of the first toe joint.

"Calcium may then deposit in the space in the joint to aggravate the problems," he said. Other problems podiatrists say are related to women's shoes are corns, callouses, inflammation of the Achilles tendon, hammertoe, general pain in the ball of the foot and "pump bump," a bone enlargement at the back of the heel bone caused by motion of the shoe against the heel bone.

Some manufacturers have responded to women's need for comfortable dress shoes. The leader in this effort is Easy Spirit, a division of United State Shoe Corporation, a major U.S. shoe manufacturer. In 1988, Easy Spirit brought to market the first dress shoe that according to its ads "looks like a pump, but feels like a sneaker." Ads for the shoe featured women in Easy Spirit heels playing basketball. The shoe, according to Claire Brinker, vice president for marketing, was built on a form of a woman's foot — not a scaled down version of a man's foot, which, she said in an interview, is commonly used by other manufacturers.

Easy Spirit shoes have been a success, said Brinker, with sales exceeding the company's expectations by seven times in the first year alone. Easy Spirit shoes now come in 14 colors, in a broad range of sizes.

Paying the Price for Fashion

Women are no longer as physically oppressed by fashion, but the cost of being fashionable oppresses women economically.

A Long Island secretary in her mid-1940s, who earns about $20,000 a year, pays about $60 a month to maintain her fingernails. Her nails are a wonder to behold, not least because she spends much of her day doing word processing. They project about one-half inch beyond her fingertips. The nails are decorated with flags, flowers, stripes or glitter — depending on the season.

Don't her nails get in the way of her typing? "Not really," she says. "I type with the nails, not my fingertips. I know they're getting too long when they hit the row of keys above the row I mean to be on. Then I get them trimmed." As an afterthought, she adds that her nails can be a problem with buttons. "This size is not too bad," she says, pointing to the medium-sized button at her throat. "But buttoning the small ones can take forever."

This secretary is not unique: nail salons populate main streets, each employing nail artists who wrap and glue silk or other materials to women's natural nails. Then they paint and decorate each one. Since fingernails are so fragile, it takes regular visits to a salon to maintain the painted nails. The cost: about $60 a month.

Women pay a high price for fashion, and this spending, when combined with their lower incomes than men, helps keep them at an economic disadvantage. "Any woman who thinks the fashion industry has her interest at heart is woefully wrong," says John Molloy in *The Woman's Dress for Success Book.* "The industry is interested in her pocketbook. And it will sell her, often at inflated prices, anything that will make money for the industry. It will sell her shoddy merchandise, and it will sell her tacky styling — anything to keep the cash register ringing."[3]

The fashion industry — through word-of-mouth, TV shows, newspapers and fashion magazines — pressures women to follow the latest fashion trends. Women are encouraged to throw out their old wardrobe and buy a new one each year, to buy the latest shades of eyeshadow and lipstick, the newest formula of anti-wrinkle skin cream, and the latest diet plan. Women find a way to stretch their budgets and buy the products and services they feel they must have.

It is not an easy economic stretch. The earnings gap between women and men is still wide, and expands as women get older. Women working full-time in 1987 earned an average of $2,000 less than men aged 18 to 24, while in the age bracket 50 to 54, women earned $16,000 less.[4] Despite these earnings gaps, women spend twice as much on clothes as men, an estimated $36.5 billion in 1992.[5]

Why Women Pay More

Adding to the cost of keeping up with changing fashion is the extra price that women pay just because their clothes were made for women and not men. Carl Priestland, chief economist for the American Apparel Association, acknowledges that essentially similar, if not identical garments — like blue jeans or knit shirts — cost more if they're intended for the women's department than the men's. In a statement prepared for this book, he wrote:

> Since the 1920s, retailers have purchased and have merchandised women's apparel differently than men's. Most of those differences are now tradition. The way women's apparel is sold to the retailer is different than men's and the retailers themselves have a different system for pricing women's apparel than men's. Even in areas where garments are unisex, like knit shirts, a shirt in the men's department will sell for less than the same knit shirt in the women's department.

One way around this discrimination is to cross the aisle and shop in the men's — or boys' — departments. Some women have been doing this for years, and enjoying the savings. And good-looking clothes do not necessarily have to cost top dollar. "When it comes to appearance, good fit can sometimes be more important than good construction," said the editors of *Consumer Reports* in an evaluation of men's and women's suits.[6]

Higher pricing for women's clothes also results from fashion changes. Men's fashions change gradually and in small ways: the width of the tie, length of the collar, the width of the lapels. Women's fashions can change dramatically from year to year, and season to season. This year, tights and stirrup pants are still in style, but the fashion pages are showing a revival of bell-bottom pants. Once they take hold, women will feel self-conscious in their stirrup pants. Favored colors also change each year, so that a woman who clings to the olive green and gold combination that was popular last year will be conspicuously out of fashion when black and red hold sway. "We will run with some items all season," said a menswear sales clerk, "whereas the women's floors often change every two weeks."

Avoiding Marketplace Perils

Focusing on quick fashion changes, manufacturers conveniently ignore the quality standards they apply to men's clothes. "Men are looking for quality goods they can wear for three or four years," said a department store salesman. And women aren't? "Women's fashions change from season to season," he said. Sometimes, the quality difference is apparent in the stitching of seams (men often have double stitched seams whereas women's are single-stitched) or the quality of the fabric. "I don't wear synthetics," said one woman, age 33, "so sometimes it is easier to buy men's clothing synthetic free than women's."

Hosiery is a good example of how lower quality can cost women more. Style dictates that women wear nylon — panty hose or stockings — that frequently run (and many women complain are uncomfortable.) The socks that men buy, however, last much longer. Lydia Justice Edwards, Idaho State Treasurer, kept all her panty hose for a year, and figured out that they cost her $520. A man who bought 24 pairs of socks a year, costing $6.50 each, would spend only $156, a difference of $364. (See "In the Market" chapter for more details.)

Both women and men are conned into paying extra money for designer-labelled clothing of questionable quality. An employee for Ralph Lauren (who previously had worked for another name designer) told us that the quality of designer clothing does not measure up to the price you pay. In fact, sometimes it is worse. Consumers should also ask themselves whether they really want to contribute to the multi-million dollar salaries earned by sports figures or celebrities from clothing with their name on it. The price of a T-shirt imprinted with the name or face of a celebrity can be twice as much as a plain one.

If the desire to be fashionable is not enough to get women to open their pocketbooks, department stores add to the temptation with store lay-out's designed to dazzle women shoppers and get them to buy on impulse. Anyone who walks in the store is immediately surrounded by products for women; the first floor is nearly always devoted primarily to cosmetics and women's accessories. "You sell more cosmetics than anything; the store would be crazy to put their best selling item behind the elevator," said a woman sales manager at a top East Coast department store. Cosmetics, she said, are the most profitable department, with women's accessories running a close second. "If you can't afford another piece of clothing, you buy cosmetics or a belt instead," she said.

In *The Beauty Myth*, Naomi Wolf accuses cosmetics manufacturers of using the techniques and language of religious cults to get women to buy vastly over-priced — and immensely profitable — products. Wolf describes what it is like for a woman to enter the cosmetic sales area of a department store:

> To reach the cosmetics counter, she must pass a deliberately disorienting prism of mirrors, lights and scents that combine to submit her to the 'sensory overload' used by hypnotists and cults to encourage suggestibility.[7]

Women typically spend from $40 to $100 every time they buy cosmetics, even when they do their buying in a drugstore. "I'm a drugstore junkie," admits a West Hartford, Connecticut woman. "I can go in there and spend $60. I like Almay and Maybelline. I even have stuff for wrinkles under my eyes, even though I'm only 35."[8]

Objective studies of cosmetics by organizations such as Consumers Union have found that there is not necessarily any correlation between price and quality, as determined by panels of testers who don't know the identity or price of the products they are using. An Olay skin cleanser that cost 85 cents an ounce was rated as high as an Elizabeth Arden cleanser at $2.13 an ounce, for example.[9] *Consumer Reports* also compared a lipstick costing nearly $15 that came in a fancy case to one costing less than $3, but which came inside a plain container. Their testers liked both about equally.[10]

Women should also be wary of paying a premium for cosmetics labelled "natural" or "hypoallergenic." There are no government standards for what these terms mean. When a manufacturer, therefore, labels a product hypoallergenic, all it means is that in its judgment the product is less likely than others to cause an allergic reaction. The Food and Drug Administration attempted to establish standards for both terms in 1975, but was blocked in court by Almay and Clinique. The companies claimed that consumers already understood that hypoallergenic products were no panacea against allergic reactions.[11]

New fashions, such as intricately decorated fingernails, impose additional costs on women. Many women used to take care of their own fingernails. All it took was a bottle of polish in the latest shade, polish remover, an emery board and a few other implements. Total investment: under $10, and the polish and remover lasted through many applications.

The Search for the Perfect Body

Cosmetics and clothes can only take women part of the way toward the fashionable look. Its the body inside the clothes that really counts today. The fashion industry tells women that they should be thin, young and large breasted. Achieving that look has become an obsession: some women religiously attend their exercise clubs seven days a week, for hours at a time; others diet themselves into illness; and still others turn for help to plastic surgeons.

Many women are overly anxious about their weight and age. The reasons elements in our society pressure women to be young and thin cut deeply into U.S. culture and the psyche of men and women. Jean Kilbourne said in an interview that "Whenever there has been a time in history when women become more powerful, the body type becomes smaller. It's as if men can barely tolerate women having power, but for women to take up space at the same time is too much." Kilbourne perceives the pressure to be thin as "greater than it's ever been."

Many women go from one quick-weight-loss scheme to another, shedding few pounds permanently, but emptying their purses all the same.

Weight loss is a big business that benefits not only the franchised weight-loss companies and the makers of high-priced mini-meals that prevent people from ever learning how to cook and eat healthy diets, but also many physicians. In 1989, for example, the Nutrition Institute of Maryland showed doctors how they could make $62,000 a year by enrolling only 15 patients on the Medifast diet plan, with each staying on the program for only 3.8 months.[12]

Fear of fat may be intertwined with fear of aging. Medical literature describes the eating disorder anorexia nervosa as "self-inflicted weight loss accompanied thereafter by a sustained avoidance of mature body shape."[13] A woman who deprives herself of food long enough will even stop menstruating. Until wrinkles or hair color threaten to give her away, a woman can look younger than her years by starving her body into looking like a pre-teenager.

In her book, *The Change*, Germaine Greer, coins a new word for the irrational fear of the old woman: anophobia. She notes that the word "old," when combined with any female noun — old woman, old girl, old cow, old bitch — is always insulting, conveying an image of "whiskery-chinned shrieking old bags in ridiculous hats, their bums stuck out in a nanny's stoop and their feet bulging with bunions."[14]

Greer asserts that "a grown woman should not have to masquerade as a girl," and reassures women that on the other side of menopause can be freedom for women who confront the fear of aging.[15]

But Greer's is a lone voice. Gloria Steinem likens the press of "fashion" images upon women to "brainwashing" which is so complete that women are not even aware they have been programmed to deny the realities of time and change. Encouraged by celebrities like Cher and Phyllis Diller, woman have gone beyond exercise and dieting to achieve the desired result. Today, they willingly pay tens of thousands of dollars and submit to dangerous surgery in their attempt to live up to the current standard of beauty. "I'm a walking billboard for cosmetic surgery," Phyllis Diller said in an interview.[16]

Avoiding Marketplace Perils

A writer for the *Los Angeles Times*, Robert Sheer, took a look inside the operating room of one of L.A.'s most prominent plastic surgeons and called it a "ghastly sight." He wrote, "A silicone chin, manufacturer size No. 2, is shoved in through the mouth, fat collected from the thigh is shot into the lips for a fuller look and the fifty-something woman now has a forty-something face for only twenty-something thousand dollars."[17]

Sheer tells us that the surgeons in this capital of cosmetic surgery do everything from ear-pinning to buttock lifts to chemical skin peels, and in the process easily become millionaires. Some are so greedy they will do procedures they know with certainty are dangerous. While the safety of silicone breast implants may not have been clear before the U.S. Food and Drug Administration (FDA) stopped almost all implants in 1992, injecting silicone directly into the face to eliminate wrinkles was known to be dangerous, but some surgeons kept on doing it anyway.

A 1992 report by a Congressional House Subcommittee, based on a three-year investigation, found that a New York City dermatologist, Dr. Norman Orentreich, had apparently injected the faces of thousands of women with silicone even though this use of the substance had never been approved by the FDA. In fact, the FDA denied approval of silicone to smooth wrinkles, scars and deep expression lines in 1976. The only permitted use was as part of a study of its safety and effectiveness for severe facial deformities. In 1979, FDA staff wrote an article describing the "swelling, discoloration, cyst formation and migration of silicone particles to the brain, lungs or heart," and in 1983 wrote a letter to the editor of *Cosmopolitan* magazine complaining about an article on the use of silicone to remove wrinkles.[18] Once injected, total removal of the silicone is impossible.

Orentreich was not the only physician defying the FDA, but had become a target because he gave speeches about his practice and had been quoted in numerous magazine articles. In addition, he apparently had a very prominent patient: First Lady Nancy Reagan. A July 24, 1984 memo by the FDA's Brooklyn District Director said, "So that you will be aware, we have reason to believe that Mrs. Nancy Reagan has been treated by Dr. Orentreich."[19]

FDA officials discussed an injunction against Dr. Orentreich, but decided in 1985 not to act. Dr. Orentreich finally signed a consent decree agreeing to stop injecting liquid silicone in February, 1992, nearly 10 years after he had received the FDA's warning. The Subcommittee's report severely criticized both the FDA and Dow Corning, the manufacturer of the silicone.

Germaine Greer argues that prejudice against older women lives on because "no one cares about older women, not even the women themselves."[20] With the baby boom population aging, women have the potential power to change the stereotypes — for themselves, and the women who come after.

Taking Charge

No legislation can free women of fashions that harm us. To raise our self-esteem so that fashion serves our needs we must look to ourselves. We need to point out to each other how we are harming our health and our pocketbooks by trying to live up to body standards that are truly unattainable for most of us. We need to nurture each other, and to give each other permission to be individuals — of all body shapes and sizes, with the wrinkles and creases we earn by our hard work and worry.

■ Don't be sucked in by the latest fad diet. Learn how to prepare food by reading cookbooks with healthy recipes, like Jane Brody's *Good Food Book* and Jean Carper's *The Food Pharmacy Cookbook*. Then eat without guilt.

■ Don't be the weight monitor for your friends and acquaintances. Noticing and commenting whenever someone drops or gains a pound contributes to obsessiveness about weight. Make your compliments general statements about how attractive or healthy the person looks.

■ Do exercise regularly, for lots of reasons, but not to the point of obsession.

■ Read Germaine Greer's book, *The Change*, and take a new look at the older women around you. Stop to think about our society's stereotypes about older women, and don't contribute to them.

■ Think deeply about your reasons for wanting cosmetic surgery. Remember, it is often dangerous and the expected "improvements" are not permanent, no matter how your surgeon may minimize the risks. Realize the surgeon has a monetary interest in convincing you the procedure is safe. If your self-esteem needs a boost, join a local chapter of the National Organization for Women, read Gloria Steinem's best-seller, *Revolution from Within*, go to school, pursue a hobby, take a risk, practice the piano — give yourself real things to feel good about.

■ Make an issue of price differences in women's and men's clothes when you spot them. Ask your local NOW chapter to do a study pricing jeans or knit shirts, and publish the results. Let your local retailers know you expect them to change their ways.

■ If you are a person who enjoys fashionable clothes and make-up, make sure your decisions to buy do not come from feelings of guilt. If the commissioned sales clerk who does a make-over on you at the cosmetics counter makes you feel uncomfortable, get up and leave with your wallet still full.

Shoes

You don't have to endure pain, and cause your own feet to become deformed, in order to wear good-looking shoes. Let your own common sense guide you, not pressure from the fashion industry.

■ For every-day use, wear heels no higher than 1 1/2 inches. This will guarantee a more normal posture. A slight heel helps relax the calf muscle.

■ Don't wear shoes with extremely pointed toes. Choose shoes that are wide enough to give your toes some room.

■ Send a message to the shoe industry by buying shoes that are comfortable.

■ Save your high heels for special occasions only, if you can't do without them, and be sure to alternate them with low heels.
Some make their high heels more comfortable by having a thin rubber sole cemented to the bottom of the shoe to cushion the balls of their feet.

Other Resources

Backlash by Susan Faludi (Crown Publishers, New York, NY, 1991, $12.50).

The Beauty Myth, by Naomi Wolf (Bantam Doubleday, New York, NY, 1991, $11).

The Food Pharmacy: Guide to Good Eating by Jean Carper (Bantam Books, New York, NY, 1991, $13.50).

Jane Brody's Good Food Book (W.W. Norton, New York, NY, 1985, $15).

Kitchen Fun for Kids by Michael Jacobson and Laura Hill (Henry Holt and Company, New York, NY, 1992, $11.95).

Avoiding Marketplace Perils

The Revolution from Within: A Book of Self Esteem by Gloria Steinem (Little Brown, New York, NY, 1992, $11.95).

No Stone Unturned: The Life and Times of Maggie Kuhn by Maggie Kuhn (Ballentine Books, New York, NY, 1991), Maggie Kuhn, founder of the Gray Panthers, began this work at 65 years of age.

Well-Being Resource For Older Americans by Ruth Fort (Moyer Bell Limited, Mt. Kisco, NY 10549, 1992).

Why Women Pay More

Appendix

HEALTH RESOURCES

AIDS Treatment Data Network
259 West 30th Street
New York, NY 10001
Provides information on AIDS
research and treatment, access to
clinical drug trials and counseling.

American Cancer Society
19 West 56th Street
New York, NY 10019
Provides pamphlets and other
information on women and cancer.
Operates the program, "Reach to
Recovery," that provides counselling
services and temporary prosthesis kits
to breast cancer patients.

**American Group Psychotherapy
Association**
25 East 21st Street, 6th Floor
New York, NY 10010
 AGPA is devoted to the development
of group psychotherapy as a mode of
treatment. Publishes information about
psychotherapy, including a consumer's
guide to psychotherapy that explains
when psychotherapy might be useful,
what criteria to use when selecting a
group and what to expect in group
psychotherapy.

American Health Care Association
1201 L Street, N.W.
Washington, D.C. 20005
Provides consumers guides on
selecting a nursing homes, including a
checklist of questions to ask.

The American Heart Association
7272 Greenville Avenue
Dallas, TX 75231-4596
Provides many free pamphlets on ways
to prevent heart disease. These
pamphlets cover such topic as women
and heart disease, women and high
blood pressure, and women and
smoking.

Arthritis Foundation
1901 Fort Myer Drive, Suite 500
Arlington, VA 22209
Supports research to find the cure for
and prevention of arthritis. Local
chapters nationwide work to improve
the quality of life for those affected by
arthritis. Provides general information
on arthritis as well as books and
videos on the subject.

**Blacks Educating Blacks About
Sexual Health Issues (BEBASHI)**
1233 Locust Street
Philadelphia, PA 19107
Provides information, counseling and
referrals on sexually transmitted
diseases and other health issues.

**Boston Women's Health Book
Collective**
P.O. Box 192
West Somerville, MA 02144
For information packages on a range
of women's health issues. Publishes
the book, *The New Our Bodies,
Ourselves.*

Avoiding Marketplace Perils

Breast Cancer Action
P.O. Box 460185
San Francisco, CA 94146
Provides support and information on
breast cancer.

Center for Medical Consumers
237 Thompson Street
New York, NY 10012
A nonprofit consumer health care
organization that provides information
on traditional and alternative health
care. Publishes *Health Facts*, a
monthly newsletter featuring in-depth
discussion on a particular health issue.
Previous newsletter subjects included,
breast cancer, infertility and
hypertension.

Community Nutrition Institute
2001 S Street, N.W., Suite 530
Washington, D.C. 20009
A non-profit consumer organization
that advocates for safe food and health
policies. Publishes a weekly
newsletter, *Nutrition Week*, which
reports on policy developments in
nutrition, hunger, homelessness and
other issues that affect consumers and
society.

Concord Feminist Health Center
38 South Main Street
Concord, NH 03301
Publishes the quarterly newsletter,
WomenWise, which covers a wide
variety of topics on women and health.

Consumer Health Services, Inc.
5720 Flatiron Parkway
Boulder, CO 80301
Operates *Prologue*, a doctor referral
service that provides information about
a doctor's credentials, experience, fee
structure, hospital affiliation and other
pertinent information to help a
consumer select a doctor.

**Chronic Fatigue Immune
Disfunction Syndrome Foundation**
965 Mission Street, Suite 425
San Francisco, CA 94103
Provides information and referrals on
CFIDS.

The DES Cancer Network
1615 Broadway
Oakland, CA 94612
Provides information and referrals on
DES. Publishes a quarterly newsletter,
DES Action Voice.

**International Childbirth Education
Associates**
P.O. Box 20048
Minneapolis, MN 55420
Provides publications on maternal and
child health. Write for their catalog,
ICA Bookmarks, which lists all of their
publications.

**International Cesarean Awareness
Network**
P.O. Box 152
Syracuse, NY 13210
Dedicated to reducing the incidence of
C-sections. Publishes a newspaper, the
Cesarean Prevention Clarion.

Livingston Foundation Medical Center
3232 Duke Street
San Diego, CA 92110
Provides information on alternative and holistic cancer therapies.

Maternity Center Association
48 East 92nd Street
New York, NY 10128
An advocacy and information organization dedicated to improving maternity care. Provides many publications including, *AIDS and Pregnancy*, *Environmental Hazards during Pregnancy* and *Preparing for Pregnancy*. The Maternity Center will provide a free catalog listing all of its publications.

Montreal Health Press
CP 1000
Station Plece DuParc
Montreal, Quebec H2W 2N1 Canada
Publishes books on menopause, sexually transmitted diseases and sexual assault.

National Abortion Rights Action League (NARAL)
1156 15th Street, N.W.
Washington, D.C. 20005
Works to protect women's right to choose, through litigation, clinic defense and supporting pro-choice candidates at all levels of government.

National Adoption Information Clearinghouse
11426 Rockville Pike, Suite 410
Rockville, MD 20852
Provides adoption information and referrals.

National Alliance of Breast Cancer Organizations
1180 Avenue of the Americas, 2nd Floor
New York, NY 10036
An advocacy organization that provides information on latest research on prevention, detection and treatment of breast cancer. Also provides referrals to services.

National Association of Childbearing Centers
3123 Gottschall Road
Perkiomenville, PA 18074
A professional organization that promotes free-standing birthing centers. Interested persons can send $1 to NACC for information on and location of birthing centers in their area.

National Black Women's Health Project
1237 Ralph Abernathy Blvd., S.W., Atlanta, GA 30310
A self-help and health advocacy group dedicated to the health and wellness of African American women. Publishes the quarterly newsletter, *Vital Signs*.

National Clearinghouse on Women and Girls with Disabilities
c/o Educational Equity Concepts, Inc.
114 East 32nd Street, N.W.
New York, NY 10016
Provides information on the special needs of women and girls with disabilities. Produces two publications, *Building Community: A Manual on Exploring Women and Disabilities* and *Bridging the Gap: A Directory of Services for Women and Girls with Disabilities.*

National Coalition for Cancer Survivorship
1010 Wayne Avenue, 5th Floor
Silver Spring, MD 20910
Operates a clearinghouse for cancer survivors and their families. Provides referrals and information on insurance, employment discrimination and psychological aspects of surviving cancer. Publishes a quarterly newsletter, *Networker.*

The National Council Against Health Fraud, Inc.
P.O. Box 1276
Loma Linda, CA 92354
A non-profit membership organization that focuses its attention upon health fraud, misinformation and quackery. Publishes *NCAFF Newsletter*, a bi-monthly newsletter that spotlights instances of health care fraud and misinformation.

National Council on Alcoholism and Drug Dependence, Inc.
12 West 21st Street
New York, NY 10001
NCADD is an education and advocacy group seeking to eradicate alcoholism and other drug addictions. It makes available, at nominal cost, fact sheets, pamphlets and reports on alcoholism and other drug addictions.

National Council on Radiation Protection and Measurements
7910 Woodmont Avenue, Suite 800
Bethesda, MD 20814
Publishes reports on radiation safety, including, control of radon in houses, a users guide to mammography, dental x-ray protection and other radiation safety topics.

National Mental Health Consumers' Self-Help Clearinghouse
Makes available articles on a wide range of mental health topics, such as, anxiety disorders, burnout, the elderly and mental health, choosing a therapist and depression.

National Osteoporosis Foundation
1150 17th Street, N.W.
Washington, D.C. 20036
Provides information on prevention and treatment of osteoporosis. Provides a free information kit, *Bonewise*, which contains preventive tips and exercises.

National Wellness Institute
A not-for-profit organization that
assists individuals and health care
professionals develop more healthy
and productive lifestyles. Sponsors an
annual wellness conference and
publishes a quarterly newsletter,
Wellness Management, which contains
information on wellness issues.

North American Vegetarian Society
Box 72
Dolgeville, NY 13329
NAVS is a non-profit educational
organization dedicated to promoting
the vegetarian way of life. Publishes
books on vegetarian philosophy, health
and nutrition, cookbooks, as well as a
quarterly newsletter, *Vegetarian Voice.*

**Nutrition for Optimal Health
Association, Inc.**
P.O. Box 380
Winnetka, IL 60093
NOHA is an educational, not-for-profit
organization seeking to promote
knowledge and use of good nutrition in
achieving and maintaining optimal
health. Provides books on nutrition and
health, as well as cassette tapes and
video rentals of NOHA wellness
seminars.

**Office on Research on Women's
Health**
National Institutes of Health
9000 Rockville Pike
Bethesda, MD 20892
Women can write for background
information on NIH research studies.

People's Medical Society
462 Walnut Street
Allentown, PA 18102
A membership organization that offers
books on Medicare, choosing a doctor,
nursing homes, lowering medical costs,
relieving pain and other health and
nutrition topics.

**The Project on Women and
Disability**
One Ashburton Place, Room 1305
Boston, MA 02108
A nonprofit organization serving
women whose lives are affected by
disability. PWD provides training,
information and referral and a
quarterly journal on women and
disability issues, called *WILDA*
(Women in Leadership/Disability
Issues).

**Public Voice for Food and Health
Policy**
1001 Connecticut Avenue, N.W.
Washington, D.C. 20036
A non-profit organization dedicated to
advancing the consumer interest in
national food and health policymaking.
Publishes reports and consumer guides
on pesticides, seafood safety, food and
nutrition policy, and cutting fat in
school lunch programs.

The Reproductive Health Technologies Project
1601 Connecticut Avenue, N.W.,
Suite 801
Washington, D.C. 20009
Promotes public education and dialogue on such contraception issues as RU-486, over-the-counter access to birth control pills and other contraception issues. Provides a booklet on RU-486.

Santa Cruz Women's Health Center
250 Locust Street
Santa Cruz, CA 95060
Provides basic information on women's health care issues.

USA Fibrositis Association
P.O. Box 1483
Dublin, OH 43017-0549
Provides information and support on fibrositis.

Women and AIDS Resource Network (WARN)
30 Third Avenue
Brooklyn, NY 11217
Counseling and referral information.

Women's Cancer Resource Center
3023 Shattuck Avenue
Berkeley, CA 94705
Provides information and referrals on women and cancer.

Women's Alcohol and Drug Education Project
c/o Women's Action Alliance
370 Lexington Avenue, Suite 603
New York, NY 10017
Provides information and materials on prevention and intervention programs.

Women's Health Action and Mobilization (WHAM)
P.O. Box 733
New York, NY 10009
A direct-action group demanding and defending reproductive freedom and quality health care for women. Contact the New York group for affiliates in other cities.

Women Healthsharing
14 Skey Lane
Toronto, Ontario, M6J 3S4 Canada
Publishes a quarterly newsletter, *Healthsharing*, which covers women health issues.

Women's Health Initiative
National Institutes of Health
Building 1, Room 260
9000 Rockville, MD 20892
Women can write for information on a long-range study of post-menopausal women and hormone replacement therapy.

CONSUMER RESOURCES

American Association of Retired Persons
601 E Street, N.W.
Washington, D.C. 20049
The nation's largest organization for people age 50 and over. AARP is involved in legislative advocacy, research and education on issues of concern to its members. Publishes many periodicals, newsletters, and other materials of interest to older Americans.

The Children's Defense Fund
CDF is dedicated to educating the nation about the needs of children. It provides a strong and effective voice for children, particularly poor, minority and disabled children. Produces a wide range of publications, including a monthly newsletter, *CDF Reports.*

Children of Aging Parents
Woodboune Office Campus, Suite 302A
1609 Woodbourne Road
Levittown, PA 19057
A support and referral organization. Publishes a bi-monthly newsletter, *Capsule.*

Compassionate Friends
P.O. Box 3696
Oak Brook, IL 60522-3696
A national self-help support group for parents who experience the death of a child. Has 660 chapters around the country.

Consumer Credit Education Foundation
919 18th Street, N.W.
Washington, D.C. 20006
Provides information on how to budget and how to cut your present expenses. Publishes *The Consumer's Almanac*, a calendar with budget charts to help keep track of your monthly income and expenses.

Consumer Federation of America
1424 16th Street, N.W., Suite 604
Washington, D.C. 20036
CFA is a national consumer advocacy organization. Its publications include a newsletter, *CFA News*, as well as case studies and pamphlets on issues ranging from health to insurance.

Consumer Information Center
P.O. Box 100
Pueblo, CO 81002
Lists free or low-cost federal government publications on a wide variety of consumer interest, including buying a new or used car, guide to car rentals, food and nutrition, health and fitness, money management and many other subjects.

Co-op America
2100 M Street, N.W., Suite 403
Washington, D.C. 20037
A membership organization that works to promote a self- reliant and sustainable quality of life. Publishes directories and catalogs that offer products for sale by businesses that care about consumers, communities and workers.

Elderhostel
75 Federal Street
Boston, MA 02110
Operates short-term, campus-based educational experiences for older adults all over the world. Publishes three seasonal catalogs.

Federal Trade Commission
Bureau of Consumer Protection
Office of Consumer
 and Business Education
6th & Pennsylvania Avenue, N.W.
Washington, D.C. 20580
 Consumers can select free or nominally priced FTC publications from their pamphlet, *Facts for Consumers and Businesses*, which catalogs the agency's most popular publications. Examples of booklets available from the FTC include guides on cosmetic surgery, diet programs, infertility services, food advertising claims, car financing scams, octane ratings, choosing and using credit cards, solving credit problems and other subjects.

Fund for the Feminist Majority
1600 Wilson Boulevard, Suite 810
Arlington, VA 22209
also
8105 West Third Street, Suite 1
Los Angeles, CA 90048
An advocacy organization seeking to get women into positions of leadership. Works on several other projects such as, reproductive rights and women and violence. Publishes a free quarterly newsletter, the *Feminist Majority Report*.

Gray Panthers
1424 16th Street, N.W., Suite 602
Washington, D.C. 20036
A nonprofit advocacy group dedicated to national health and other issues of concern to older adults. Publishes the quarterly newsletter, *Gray Panthers Network*.

National Center for Financial Education
P.O. Box 34070
San Diego, CA 92163-4070
A nonprofit education organization dedicated to helping people plan for their financial futures. Provides do-it-yourself kits on repairing your line of credit, obtaining and interpreting your credit file, spending and savings techniques and other important consumer credit subjects.

National Citizens' Coalition for Nursing Home Reform
1224 M Street N.W., Suite 301
Washington, D.C. 20005
A coalition of nursing home residents and their families devoted to improving nursing home care. Provides information on how to select a nursing home.

National Clearinghouse for the Defense of Battered Women
125 South 9th Street, Suite 302
Reading, PA 19107
Provides information and technical assistance to battered women who have been charged with homicide or assault offenses involving their abusers.

National Clearinghouse on Marital and Date Rape
Women's History Research Center
2325 Oak Street
Berkeley, CA 94708
Provides information and phone consultations concerning rape.

National Consumers League
815 15th Street, N.W.
Washington, D.C. 20005
The nation's oldest consumer organization, NCL represents the consumer viewpoint before Congress and federal regulatory agencies. Publishes the *NCL Bulletin*, a bi-monthly newsletter on consumer issues. In addition, NCL publishes several consumer guides on such topics as prescription drugs, women and AIDS, renters insurance, telemarketing fraud and other subjects.

The National Council on the Aging
409 Third Street, S.W.
Washington, D.C. 20024
NOCA serves as a national resource for information, research and advocacy on every aspect of aging. Provides free pamphlets concerning the elderly and smoking, diet, prescription drugs, fitness, depression alcohol.

National Displaced Homemakers Network
1625 K Street, N.W.
Washington, D.C. 20006
provides information and referrals on displaced homemakers. Publishes a quarterly newsletter *Network News.*

National Women's Law Center
1616 P Street, N.W.
Washington, D.C. 20036
Lobbies and advocates for equality of women.

HEALTH & CONSUMER TOLL-FREE HOTLINES

How to Use the Toll-Free Hotline Directory

The toll-free hotline directory is sub-divided into two categories: Health and Consumer Issues. Within each category, the organizations offering toll-free services are listed alphabetically by name. Please be aware that some toll-free listings may be inaccessible from within their state of origin.

Although a few toll-free lines are equipped to respond to individual problems on a personal level, the main purpose of a large majority of hotlines is to provide information and local referrals. Be sure to have a pen and paper on hand.

Health Hotlines

ABORTION HOTLINE/ NATIONAL ABORTION FEDERATION
Counseling and medical guidelines for quality abortion care and referrals to member clinics. Available 9:30 am to 5:30 pm EST Monday-Friday.
800-772-9100
except DC, AK, HI 202-667-5881

AIDS HOTLINE
Recorded message explains symptoms, means of transmission and high risk categories; gives address for brochure, *Facts About AIDS*, and other publications. Operated by the Center for Disease Control. Available 24 hours, 7 days a week.
800-342-AIDS (in English)
800-342-SIDA (in Spanish)

AL-ANON FAMILY GROUP
Provides information on alcoholism specifically aimed at the families of alcoholics. Referrals to local chapters. Available 24 hours, 7 days a week.
800-356-9996
except NY 212-245-3151

ALZHEIMER'S ASSOCIATION
Sends out free literature on Alzheimer's Disease and refers callers to local chapters. Available 9 am to 5 pm CST, Monday-Friday.
800-621 -0379
except, IL 800-572-6037

AMERICAN ACADEMY OF ALLERGY AND IMMUNOLOGY
Asthma and allergies information and physician referral. Provides booklets on asthma and allergies. Available 24 hours, 7 days a week.
800-822-ASMA

AMERICAN MEDICAL CENTER CANCER INFORMATION LINE
Information on cancer prevention, detection, diagnosis, treatment and rehabilitation; free professional counseling of patients, family members and friends, to help callers cope with life-threatening illness; sends free literature. Available 8:30 am to 5 pm MST, Monday-Friday.
800-525-3777
except CO 303-233-6501

AMERICAN COUNCIL ON ALCOHOLISM
A coalition of local, state, regional and national groups which seeks to end alcohol abuse and alcoholism through public education and employee assistance programs. Available 24 hours, 7 days a week.
800-527-5344
except MD 301-296-5555

AMERICAN DIABETES ASSOCIATION
Provides information and referrals to local support groups.
800-ADA-DISC
except VA & DC metro area
703-549-1500

AMERICAN INSTITUTE FOR PREVENTIVE MEDICINE
Provides information about programs to stop smoking, reduce stress, control weight and other issues of health education. Available 8 am to 4:30 pm EST, Monday—Friday.
800-345-AIPM

AMERICAN KIDNEY FUND
Assists kidney patients who are unable to pay treatment costs; provides information on kidney-related diseases and donating organs. Available 8am to 5 pm EST, Monday—Friday.
800-638-8299
except MD 800-492-8361

AMERICAN SOCIETY FOR PSYCHOPROPHYLAXIS IN OBSTETRICS
Non-profit organization concerned with Lamaze childbirth preparation and family-centered maternity care; teacher and physician referral service. Available 9 am to 5 pm EST, Monday-Friday.
800-368-4404
except VA 703-524-7802

AMERICAN TRAUMA SOCIETY
Offers professional counseling, public education, and information on trauma. Available 9 am to 5 pm EST, Monday-Friday.
800-556-7890

ARTHRITIS MEDICAL CENTER
Sends information on the Holistic
Approach to the treatment of Arthritis.
Available 9 am to 3 pm EST,
Monday-Friday.
800-327-3027

**ASTHMA-LUNG DISEASE
HOTLINE**
Answers questions about asthma,
emphysema, chronic bronchitis,
tuberculosis and occupational and
environmental lung diseases. Questions
answered by registered nurses or other
health professionals. Sponsored by the
National Jewish Center for
Immunology and Respiratory
Medicine. Available 8 am to 5 pm
MST, Monday—Friday.
800-222-LUNG
except Denver 303-355-LUNG

**BETTER HEARING
INSTITUTE/HEARING HELPLINE**
Provides information about hearing
loss, noise pollution, doctors and
hearing aid specialists in the caller's
local area. Available 9 am to 5 pm
EST, Monday-Friday.
800-EAR-WELL
800-424-8576

**CHILDREN'S HOSPICE
INTERNATIONAL**
Provides support system, resource
sharing and information to health care
professionals, families and other
hospice organizations which offer care
to terminally ill children.
800-2424453
except VA 703-684-0330

**CONSUMER DIVISION OF
AMERICAN SPEECH,
LANGUAGE, AND HEARING
ASSOCIATION**
Provides general information on
speech, language and hearing disorders
as well as referrals for all ages.
Translations from Spanish to English
available. Available 8:30 am to 4:30
pm EST, Monday-Friday.
800-638-8255

**DIAL-A-HEARING SCREENING
TEST**
Tells where to call in your area for a
free hearing screening test. Offers
numbers for self-help groups.
Available 9 am to 6 pm EST,
Monday-Friday.
800-222-EARS
PA 800-345-EARS

**DRUG ABUSE INFORMATION
AND REFERRAL
LINE/NATIONAL INSTITUTE ON
DRUG ABUSE**
Provides information and referral.
Offers a Spanish/ English hotline and
information on AIDS and high risk
behavior. Available 9 am to 3 am
EST, Monday-Friday; also weekends
from 12 noon to 3 am.
800-6624357
800-66-AYUDA

ENDOMETRIOSIS ASSOCIATION

Recorded message asks callers to leave their address for information mailings. Available 24 hours a day, 7 days a week.
800-992-ENDO
except WI 414-962-8972

HEADACHE FOUNDATION

Information on possible causes, treatments and prevention of all types of headaches; makes referrals to local physicians. Available 8 am to 5 pm CST, Monday—Friday.
800-843-2256
except IL 800-523-8858

HILL-BURTON FREE HOSPITAL CARE

Sponsored by the Department of Health and Human Services. Sends information to callers about free care in hospitals and other health facilities, including a list of facilities in the caller's local area that participate in the program; advises callers on how to file a complaint about the program. Service is primarily for low-income people to cover the costs of medical care. Available 9:30 am to 5:30 pm EST, Monday-Friday. Monitored by an answering machine all other times.
800-638-0742
except MD 800-492-0359

HOSPICE-LINK/HOSPICE EDUCATION INSTITUTE

Provides a directory of hospices and local referral, answers general questions on principles and practices of the group, and lends a sympathetic ear. Available 9 am to 5 pm EST, Monday-Friday.
800-331-1620

MEAT AND POULTRY HOTLINE

Provides safety hints on the proper handling, preparation, storing and cooking of meat, poultry and eggs. Sponsored by the U.S. Department of Agriculture. Available 10 am to 4 pm EST, Monday-Friday.
800-535-4555

MOTHERS AGAINST DRUNK DRIVERS (MADD)

Provides counseling, victim hotline, and nearest chapter referrals. Sends out literature. 24 hour service.
800-438-6233
except TX 817-268-6233

NATIONAL CENTER FOR STUTTERING

Free information to parents of children who stutter; treatment workshop (for a fee) for older children and adults who stutter; and training sessions for therapists on the latest techniques. Available 9 am to 5 pm EST, Monday-Friday.
800-221-2483
except NY 212-532-1460

Avoiding Marketplace Perils

NATIONAL COUNCIL ON ALCOHOLISM
Provides information on alcoholism and makes referrals to local affiliates. Available 24 hours, 7 days a week.
800-NCA-CALL

NATIONAL DOWN SYNDROME SOCIETY
Answers questions and sends information on Down Syndrome; refers callers to resources in their communities. Available 9 am to 5 pm EST, Monday-Friday. Other times monitored by machine.
800-221 4602
except NY 212-460-9330

NATIONAL FOUNDATION FOR DEPRESSIVE ILLNESS
A recorded message describes symptoms of depression and gives an address for more information and physician referral. Available 24 hours, 7 days a week.
800-248-4344

NATIONAL INFORMATION CENTER ON ORPHAN DRUGS AND RARE DISEASES
Answers questions about orphan drugs and inquiries on rare diseases. Sponsored by the Federal Office of Orphan Product Development/the Food and Drug Administration. Available 9 am to 5 pm EST, Monday-Friday.
800-456-3505

ORGAN DONOR HOTLINE
Offers information and referrals for organ donation and transplant. Answers requests for organ donor cards. Available 24 hours, seven days a week.
800-24-DONOR

ORTON DYSLEXIA SOCIETY
Clearinghouse for information on dyslexia. Offers information on testing and tutoring. Available 9 am to 5 pm EST, Monday-Friday.
800-ABCD-123

SECOND OPINION HOTLINE FOR NON-EMERGENCY SURGERY
A project of U.S. Department of Health and Human Services' Health-Care Finance Administration; provides free referrals to specialists to double-check advice before an operation (fee for 2nd opinion may be covered by insurance). Available 8 am to 12 am EST, seven days a week.
800-638-6833
except MD 800-492-6603

SEXUALLY TRANSMITTED DISEASE HOTLINE
Sponsored by the American Social Health Association. A confidential, anonymous, free consultation, information and clinic referral service on all aspects of sexually transmitted diseases. (Note: line is often busy.) Available 8 am to 6 pm EST, Monday-Friday.
800-227-8922

**SUDDEN INFANT DEATH
SYNDROME INSTITUTE**
Provides information on research,
patient care, and support groups.
Physicians available for advice.
Available 8 am to 4:30 pm EST,
Monday-Friday.
800-232-SIDS

**TERRI GOTTHELF LUPUS
RESEARCH INSTITUTE**
Offers information on lupus, including
a list of centers that conduct research
and provide health services to lupus
patients. Available 9 am to 7 pm EST,
Monday-Friday.
800-82-LUPUS
except CT 203-852-0120

THE LIVING BANK
Information and registry for people to
donate their organs, tissues, bones or
bodies for transplant or research.
Available 24 hours, 7 days a week.
800-528-2971
except TX 713-528-2971

**UNITED SCLERODERMA
FOUNDATION**
Chapters in various states; provides
brochures, books, and a newsletter to
members. Available 8 am to 5 pm
PST, Monday-Friday.
800-722-4673

**U.S. DEPARTMENT OF HEALTH
AND HUMAN SERVICES/OFFICE
OF DISEASE PREVENTION AND
HEALTH
PROMOTION-HEALTHY OLDER
PEOPLE PROGRAM**
Makes referrals to state resources;
provides consumer materials on
behavioral changes designed to
improve the health of older people.
Available 9 am to 5 pm EST,
Monday-Friday.
800-3364797
except MD 301-565-4167

**U.S. DEPARTMENT OF HEALTH
AND HUMAN
SERVICES OFFICE OF THE
INSPECTOR GENERAL (OIG) -
MEDICARE**
Handles complaints on evidence of
fraud or abuse in Medicare and
Medicaid programs; answers questions
about Medicare coverage. Available 24
hours.
800-368-5779
except MD 301-597-0724

**U.S. PHARMACOPEIA,
PROBLEM REPORTING
PROGRAM**
Distributes educational and
informational material concerning
medical devices; consumers
dissatisfied with medical self-test
products may contact this number.
Available 9 am to 4:30 pm EST,
Monday-Friday. Taped and monitored
at other times.
800-638-6725
except MD 301-881-0256

Consumer Hotlines

AMERICAN SOCIETY OF APPRAISERS
Provides information on appraisal of fine arts, antiques, gems and jewelry, and real estate. Available 9 am to 5 pm EST, Monday-Friday.
800-ASA-VALU

AT&T SPECIAL NEEDS CENTER
Provides service and equipment to hearing, speech, motion or vision impaired individuals. Sells and services telephone equipment at cost. Available 8:30 am to 7 pm EST, Monday-Friday.
800-233-1222

AUTO SAFETY HOTLINE/NATIONAL HIGHWAY TRAFFIC SAFETY ADMINISTRATION
Provides information on safety recalls and defects on automobiles. Monitored by answering machine, leave request and NHTSA will call back. Available 8 am to 5:30 pm EST, Monday-Friday.
800-424-9393
except DC 202-366-0123

CIVIL RIGHTS HOTLINE
Accepts calls regarding discrimination on the basis of race, color, national origin, handicap or age occurring in Health & Human Services programs; e.g. in admission, service or access in hospitals, nursing homes, day care centers or state health care assistance. Available 9 am to 5:30 pm EST, Monday-Friday.
800-368-1019

CONSUMER EDUCATION RESEARCH CENTER
Non-profit consumer protection organization which publishes consumer education materials on issues such as veteran's benefits and social security benefits for use by the public, schools and libraries.
800-872-0121

CONSUMER PRODUCT SAFETY COMMISSION
Receives reports on injuries/deaths from hazardous manufactured products; provides information on recalls and product safety. Information is recorded and a touchtone phone is required for access. Available 24 hours, 7 days a week.
800-638-CPSC

FEDERAL DEPOSIT INSURANCE CORPORATION
Information on Truth-in-Lending Act, Equal Credit Opportunity Act, Fair Credit Reporting Act and other banking laws; handles banking and housing complaints. Available 8 am to 4:30 pm EST, Monday-Friday.
800-654-9198

FEDERAL TAX INFORMATION
Internal Revenue Service answers
federal tax questions; helps set up
installment agreements for those who
cannot afford to meet payments in a
lump sum; resolves problems with
W-2 forms; directs callers to free tax
preparation classes during filing
season; low-income and elderly callers
can obtain volunteer help preparing tax
forms year-round. Available 8 am to
4:30 pm EST, Monday-Friday.
800-829-1040
AK & HI 800-428-4732
except DC 202-488-3100

**FUNERAL SERVICE CONSUMER
ARBITRATION PROGRAM**
Sponsored by the National Funeral
Directors Association. Helps to solve
disputes between consumers and
directors (mostly contractual). Will
send literature upon request.
Available 9 am to 5 pm EST,
Monday-Friday.
800-662-7666

**HEATH (HIGHER EDUCATION
AND ADULT TRAINING FOR
PEOPLE WITH HANDICAPS)**
Sponsored by the American Council
on Education. Offers information about
post-secondary education options open
to handicapped individuals. Available
8:45 am to 4:45 pm EST,
Monday-Friday.
800-544-3284
except DC 202-939-9320

**HOME OWNERS WARRANTY
CORPORATION**
Offers free dispute settlement program
for homeowners in which H.O.W.
builders (not homeowners) are bound
by the decision of the mediator.
Available 8:30 am to 5:30 pm EST,
Monday-Friday.
800-CALL-HOW
except DC 202-463-4600

INVESTMENT HOTLINE
Sponsored by the National Credit
Union Administration. Provides
information on investments relating to
credit unions. Available 12 noon to 5
pm EST, Monday-Friday.
800-755-5999
except DC 202-682-9640

**MAJOR APPLIANCE CONSUMER
ACTION PANEL**
Funded by industry. Helps consumers
of kitchen and laundry appliances, air
conditioners, etc. resolve complaints if
they have been unable to get
satisfaction from the manufacturer.
Independent mediation panel offers
nonbinding decision; hotline supplies
MACAP address for written inquiries.
800-621-0477
except IL 312-984-5858

NATIONAL COUNCIL ON THE AGING

National information and consulting center for the aged. Available 9 am to 5 pm EST, Monday-Friday. Library is open to the public Tuesday - Friday.
800-424-9046
except DC 202-497-1200

NATIONAL INSTITUTE FOR OCCUPATIONAL SAFETY AND HEALTH

Answers questions relating to NIOSH policies and occupational safety and health. Available 8 am to 4:30 pm EST, Monday-Friday. Answering machine during off hours.
800-35-NIOSH
except GA 404-329-3061

NATIONAL ORGANIZATION OF SOCIAL SECURITY CLAIMANTS REPRESENTATIVES

A non-profit group which provides addresses of attorneys in caller's area who specialize in claims against the Social Security Administration; most member attorneys work on a contingency basis. Available 9 am to 5 pm EST, Monday-Friday.
800-431-2804

OFFICE OF CONSUMER AFFAIRS/U.S. DEPARTMENT OF COMMERCE

Handles complaints and inquiries from the general public, including allegations of fraud, waste, abuse and mismanagement within the department. Usually answered by machine.
800-424-5197
except DC 202-377-2495
EMERGENCY 202-377-0907

OLDER WOMEN'S LEAGUE (OWL) POWER LINE

A national membership organization concerned about the problems of midlife and older women. Reports on current studies and congressional and federal actions affecting women.
800-825-3695

RIGHT-TO KNOW HOTLINE

Provides assistance regarding the Right-to-Know Act which requires community notification about chemical storage and spills. Run by Geo-Resource Consultants (a private non-government group). Available 8:30 am to 5 pm EST, Monday-Friday.
800-535-0202
except D.C. 202-479-2449

TELE-CONSUMER HOTLINE
Answers questions on long-distance options and service, telephone equipment and repairs, ways to cut costs, and where to get help resolving billing problems. Founded by the Telecommunications Research and Action Center and the Consumer Federation of America. Available 9 am to 5 pm EST, Monday-Friday.
800-332-1124
except DC 202-223-4371

U.S. CONSUMER PRODUCT SAFETY COMMISSION/OFFICE OF INFORMATION AND PUBLIC AFFAIRS
Independent federal agency which serves to protect the public from unreasonable risks of injury from consumer products. Available 9 am to 5 pm EST, Monday-Friday.
800-638-CPSC
TTY 800-638-8270
MD 800-492-8104

U.S. DEPARTMENT OF EDUCATION-EDUCATION RESOURCES CENTER CLEARINGHOUSE ON ADULT, CAREER AND VOCATIONAL EDUCATION
Resources available on educational concerns; list of program and publications. Available 8 am to 5 pm EST, Monday-Friday.
800-848-4815
except Ohio 614-486-3655

WOMEN'S SPORTS FOUNDATION
Educational non-profit group provides answers to questions about women's sports and fitness matters including pregnancy and exercise, history of women's sports, where to get involved and internship programs. Available 9 am to 5 pm EST, Monday-Friday.
800-227-3988
except NY 212-972-9170

Avoiding Marketplace Perils

WHAT KILLS THE MOST WOMEN?*
(deaths per 100,000 women in 1989)

Age	Heart Disease	Breast Cancer	All Cancers
45-54	34	45	152
55-64	428	111	373
65-74	428	111	671
75-84	1,360	148	1,010
85+	4,242	189	1,313

Coronary heart disease kills far more women than breast cancer... if you combine all age groups. But it's not until women reach their mid-1970s that deaths from heart disease far outstrip breast cancer deaths. And the risk of heart disease at younger ages may be considerably lower for health-conscious women...

[*Reprinted from the *Nutrition Action Healthletter*, November, 1992.]

BREAST IMPLANT RESOURCES

COMMAND TRUST NETWORK
Kathleen Anneken (Augmentation Division)
P.O. Box 17082
Covington, KY 41017
(606) 331-0055

Sybil Goldrich (Reconstruction Division)
256 South Linden Dr.
Beverly Hills, CA 90212
(213) 556-1738/9 or 271-5000

**NATIONAL WOMEN'S HEALTH
NETWORK**
1325 G Street N.W., Lower Level
Washington, D.C. 20005
(202) 347-1140

**BOSTON WOMEN'S HEALTH BOOK
COLLECTIVE**
P.O. Box 192
West Sommerville, MA 02144
(617) 625-0271
(Information packet for a $10.00 donation)

FOOD AND DRUG ADMINISTRATION
Breast Implant Information
HFE-88 5600 Fishers Lane
Rockville, MD 20857
(301) 443-3170

**FOR ADDITIONAL SCLERODERMA
INFORMATION
SCLERODERMA SOCIETY**
1182 Teaneck Road
Teaneck, NJ 07666
(201) 837-9826
Call the society for more information on
local chapters.

IMPLANT MANUFACTURERS
Baxter Healthcare Corporation
1 Baxter Parkway
Deerfield, IL 60015
1-800-323-4533

Bioplasty Inc.
1385 Centennial Drive
St. Paul, MN 55113
1-800-328-9105

Dow Corning Corporation
P.O. Box 994
Midland, MI 48686-0994
1-800-442-5442

McGhan Medical Inc.
700 Ward Drive
Santa Barbara, CA 93111
1-800-624-4261

Mentor
5425 Hollister Avenue
Santa Barbara, CA 93111
1-800-525-9151

Porex Technologies
500 Bohannon Road
Fairburn, GA 30213
1-800-241-0195

Surgitek
3037 Mt. Pleasant Street
Racine, WI 53404
1-800-634-4397

Cox-Uphoff (CUI Corporation)
1035 Cindy Lane
Carpinteria, CA 93103
1-800-872-4749

PHYSICIAN GROUPS
American Society of Plastic and
Reconstruction Surgeons
444 E. Algonquin Road
Arlington Heights, IL 60005
1-800-635-0635
This group has publicly stated that they will
find a plastic surgeon to assist any patient
with implant problems.

American Academy of Cosmetic Surgery
159 East Live Oak Avenue
Suite 204
Arcadia, CA 91006
1-800-221-9808

Why Women Pay More

FACTS FOR CONSUMERS*
Infertility Services

About one in six U.S. couples is infertile. If you are among them, you may have considered contacting a health care provider that offers advanced infertility services.

Most infertility service providers will tell you what their record has been in helping couples. But in talking with or writing to different providers, you may find that success rates are calculated differently — making it confusing to select among the more than 200 programs offering these advanced services.

In addition, a particular infertility service may have a lower success rate than others, but specialize in more difficult cases. Or, a service may have a very good overall success rate, but not be the best one to treat your particular problem. Infertility experts emphasize that your chances for success depend on many factors, such as age and cause of infertility.

The staff at the Federal Trade Commission has reviewed how success-rate claims are calculated by infertility services. The following information may help in evaluating these claims and selecting the best program for your specific needs.

How Success Rates are Advertised
As you contact infertility service providers, consider carefully how success rates are calculated. Make sure to ask for the success rate for people who fit your particular patient profile, such as your age and cause of infertility.

Ask which specific procedures are included or omitted in the figures. This information can be difficult to understand, so ask for it in "plain English."

Included here are explanations of some frequently used success-rate calculations. For help in understanding these definitions, please refer to *"Terms You Need to Know."*

Live Birth Rate per Egg Stimulation
This figure tells how many births occurred in relation to the number of egg-stimulation procedures performed. Experts say this figure is the most meaningful overall success-rate statistic, because it includes live births as well as all procedures performed, including those that failed.

Avoiding Marketplace Perils

Live Birth Rate per Embryo Transfer

This figure refers to the percentage of births from all embryo transfer procedures. Although this number reflects live births — which may be the most meaningful figure — it does not include those instances where the attempt at egg stimulation, egg retrieval, and fertilization did not succeed.

Pregnancy Rate per Attempted Egg Stimulation

This rate refers to the number of clinical pregnancies resulting from all egg-stimulation attempts. This figure does not tell you whether these pregnancies resulted in live births, but does include the women who received multiple treatments.

Pregnancy Rate per Woman in the Program

This rate refers to how many clinical pregnancies occurred per woman in the program. Excluded from this figure are the number of births and the number of times an individual woman may have undergone the procedure prior to achieving a pregnancy.

Terms You Need To Know

In vitro fertilization (IVF): In this procedure, a woman's eggs are retrieved and combined with sperm to fertilize in the laboratory. Any fertilized eggs, called embryos, are returned to the uterus.

> The steps involved in IVF are:
> Step 1 Egg Stimulation
> Step 2 Egg Retrieval
> Step 3 Fertilization
> Step 4 Embryo Transfer

> If all goes well, the next two steps are:
> Step 5 Clinical Pregnancy
> Step 6 Live Birth

Gamete intrafallopian transfer (GIFT). This procedure differs from IVF in that retrieved eggs and sperm are injected into a woman's fallopian tubes where fertilization can take place.

Because fertilization does not take place outside the body, there is no embryo transfer step in GIFT.

Egg Stimulation: This refers to the administration of fertility drugs to a woman to "stimulate" and increase egg production.

Egg Retrieval: This process involves the removal of an egg or eggs from the ovaries and follicles for subsequent fertilization through IVF or GIFT.

Fertilization: The retrieved egg is mixed with sperm, after which the egg becomes fertilized and forms what then becomes an embryo.

Embryo Transfer: After an egg and sperm fertilize in the laboratory, the newly formed embryo is transferred to the uterus.

Clinical Pregnancy: This is a pregnancy which has been confirmed by ultrasound or other clinical means. Prior to this point, a blood test or a urinary pregnancy test *may* indicate a pregnancy. Such tests look for human chorionic gonadotropin or HCG. If the blood or urinary tests indicate a positive reading, then the pregnancy is referred to as a"chemical pregnancy." Infertility service providers generally do not accept chemical pregnancies as anything more than an indicator because conditions other than pregnancy can account for a positive reading.

Live Birth: This refers to the actual live birth of one or more babies. In determining success-rate data using live births, the industry standard is to count a "live birth" as a single delivery, regardless of how many babies were born.

Pregnancy Rate per Attempted Egg Retrieval
This rate reflects the number of clinical pregnancies resulting from all egg-retrieval attempts. This statistic does not tell whether these pregnancies resulted in live births and does not include instances where egg stimulation did not produce an egg to retrieve.

Pregnancy Rate per Embryo Transfer
This usually refers to how many clinical pregnancies occurred in relation to the number of embryo-transfer procedures performed. This figure does not say how many births occurred or how successful the program was in stimulating egg production, in obtaining egg retrieval, and in fertilizing eggs retrieved.

It takes time for new infertility service providers to establish success rates based on live births. For this reason, some providers cite only national statistics in discussing success rates. Be wary of any claims not based on a provider's own experience. Experts say it is fair for new providers to report anticipated births by including those pregnancies that have progressed beyond 26 weeks — at which point the pregnancy is highly likely to continue to term.

Some providers also favor reporting "cumulative" pregnancy and birth rate claims. Cumulative rates suggest the overall probability of a pregnancy or birth occurring based on women undergoing several successive procedures. You may want to ask how such calculations are made and what percentage of patients were able to go through multiple treatments. Evaluate all claims of success carefully.

How to Select an Infertility Service

You may want to begin your search for fertility specialists by asking your gynecologist, obstetrician, family doctor, or friends and relatives for recommendations. Ask your local hospital or medical society for names. In addition, you may want to contact local infertility support groups, which can provide you with both information and emotional support.

Plan to talk with several providers of infertility services before taking any particular course of action. By doing so, you can compare programs, gain more information about the field, and learn about different treatments applicable to your situation.

You may want to contact infertility programs first by telephone, study any literature sent to you and, then, visit those that most interest you. Try to select an infertility provider that you feel comfortable with and is convenient for you. Here are some questions to ask providers.

What is your infertility service's success rate and how is it calculated? *For established programs*: **What is your live birth rate per egg stimulation attempted?** *For new programs*: **What is your live birth rate plus ongoing pregnancies past 26 weeks per egg stimulation?**

You will want to examine how each infertility service tabulates its success rate and consider how meaningful these figures are.

What is your success rate with couples who have problems similar to ours?

Most importantly, find out how successful an infertility service has been in helping couples with your specific problems. Tell the staff your individual circumstances. Then ask: "Given our particular medical history, what are our chances of having a baby after undergoing a single egg-stimulation procedure?"

How long has your infertility service been in existence? How many patients have you treated? What is the specific training of your medical personnel?

You probably will want to select a program that is well-established, has worked with many patients, and has a highly-trained medical staff.

Is your infertility service associated with a medical board specializing in infertility?

You may wish to determine whether the infertility service has a doctor who is board-certified by the American Board of Obstetrics and Gynecology in the subspecialty of Reproductive Endocrinology. This board certification provides recognition of tested expertise in IVF and GIFT procedures.

Can you send me written material about the particular procedure you are recommending?

It is helpful to get written information about any medical procedures you may undergo. IVF and GIFT treatments should be explained to you in detail so that you fully understand the nature of these procedures.

What are the fees for these procedures? How much will drugs cost? What is typically covered by insurance?

Costs for infertility procedures are relatively expensive, and coverage by health insurance plans varies. Ask the cost of each step in the IVF or GIFT procedure. Most infertility services charge you as you advance through each step of the procedure rather than require a payment-in-fill prior to the start of a treatment. You should review your health insurance to see which parts, if any, of the IVF or GIFT procedures are covered and discuss the matter with the provider of your choice.

Can we talk with several former or current patients who have had problems similar to ours?

Talking with a provider's patients can help in confirming your impressions of an infertility program, particularly the way in which patients are treated. You frequently can get an idea of a program's strengths and weaknesses from those who have participated in it.

Where to Go for More Information

For help in researching or checking possible complaints about particular infertility programs, you may want to contact the state medical board or county medical society. For more information about infertility, write to the American Fertility Society (2140 Eleventh Avenue South, Suite 200, Birmingham, Alabama 35205-2800). In addition, an infertility support group such as RESOLVE, with national headquarters in Arlington, Massachusetts and numerous local chapters, may be of immediate help to you. If you have further questions or want to discuss possible problems about this issue, contact the FTC at (202) 326-3123 or write to the Division of Service Industry Practices, Federal Trade Commission, Washington, D.C. 20580. Although the FTC does not usually intervene in individual cases, the information you provide may indicate a pattern of possible law violations requiring action by the Commission. [Reprinted from the FTC's *Facts for Consumers: Infertility Services*, March 1990]

Avoiding Marketplace Perils

THE FACTS ABOUT WEIGHT LOSS PRODUCTS AND PROGRAMS*

The Weight-Loss Industry

Looking for a quick and easy way to lose weight? You're not alone. An estimated 50 million Americans will go on diets this year. And while some will succeed in taking off weight, very few — *perhaps 5 percent* — will manage to keep all of it off in the long run.

One reason for the low success rate is that many people look for quick and easy solutions to their weight problems. They find it hard to believe in this age of scientific innovations and medical miracles that an effortless weight-loss method doesn't exist.

So they succumb to quick-fix claims like "Eat All You Want and Still Lose Weight!" or Melt Fat Away — While You Sleep!" And they invest their hopes (and their money) in all manner of pills, potions, gadgets, and programs that hold the promise of a slimmer, happier future.

The weight-loss business is a booming industry. Americans spend an estimated $30 billion a year on all types of diet programs and products, including diet foods and drinks. Trying to sort out all of the competing claims — often misleading, unproven or just plain false — can be confusing and costly.

This brochure is designed to give you the facts behind the claims, to help you avoid the outright scams, and to encourage you to consider thoroughly the costs and the consequences of the dieting decisions you make.

The Facts About Weight Loss

Being obese can have serious health consequences. These include an increased risk of heart disease, stroke, high blood pressure, diabetes, gallstones, and some forms of cancer. Losing weight can help reduce these risks. Here are some general points to keep in mind:

Any claims that you can lose weight effortlessly are false. The only proven way to lose weight is either to reduce the number of calories you eat or to increase the number of calories you burn off through exercise. Most experts recommend a combination of both.

Very low-calorie diets are not without risk and should be pursued only under medical supervision. Unsupervised very low-calorie diets can deprive you of important nutrients and are potentially dangerous.

Fad diets rarely have any permanent effect. Sudden and radical changes in your eating patterns are difficult to sustain over time. In addition, so-called "crash" diets often send dieters into a cycle of quick weight loss, followed by a "rebound" weight gain once normal eating resumes, and even more difficulty reducing when the next diet is attempted.

To lose weight safely and keep it off requires long-term changes in daily eating and exercise habits. Many experts recommend a goal of losing about a pound a week. A modest reduction of 500 calories per day will achieve this goal, since a total reduction of 3,500 calories is required to lose one pound of fat. An important way to lower your calorie intake is to learn and practice healthy eating habits.

In Search of the "Magic Bullet"

Some dieters peg their hopes on pills and capsules that promise to "burn," "block," "flush," or otherwise eliminate fat from the system. But science has yet to come up with a low-risk "magic bullet" for weight loss. Some pills may help control the appetite, but they can have serious side effects. (Amphetamines, for instance, are highly addictive and can have an adverse impact on the heart and central nervous system.) Other pills are utterly worthless.

The Federal Trade Commission (FTC) and a number of state Attorneys General have successfully brought cases against marketers of pills claiming to absorb or burn fat. The Food and Drug Administration (FDA) has banned 111 ingredients once found in over-the-counter diet products. None of these substances, which include alcohol, caffeine, dextrose, and gum, have proved effective in weight-loss or appetite suppression. Beware of the following products that are touted as weight-loss wonders:

Diet patches, which are worn on the skin, have not been proven to be safe or effective. The FDA has seized millions of these products from manufacturers and promoters.

"Fat blockers" purport to physically absorb fat and mechanically interfere with the fat a person eats.

"Starch blockers" promise to block or impede starch digestion. Not only is the claim unproven, but users have complained of nausea, vomiting, diarrhea, and stomach pains.

"Magnet" diet pills allegedly "flush fat out of the body." The FTC has brought legal action against several marketers of these pills.

Glucomannan is advertised as the "Weight Loss Secret That's Been in the Orient for Over 500 Years." There is little evidence supporting this plant root's effectiveness as a weight-loss product.

Some *bulk producers or fillers*, such as fiber-based products, may absorb liquid and swell in the stomach, thereby reducing hunger. Some fillers, such as guar gum, can even prove harmful, causing obstructions in the intestines, stomach, or esophagus. The FDA has taken legal action against several promoters of products containing guar gum.

Spirulina, a species of blue-green algae, has not been proven effective for losing weight.

Phony Devices and Gadgets

Phony weight-loss devices range from those that are simply ineffective to those that are truly dangerous to your health. At minimum, they are a waste of your hard-earned money. Some of the fraudulent gadgets that have been marketed to hopeful dieters over the years include:

"Electrical muscle stimulators" have legitimate use in physical therapy treatment. But the FDA has taken a number of them off the market because they were promoted for weight loss and body toning. When used incorrectly, muscle stimulators can be dangerous, causing electrical shocks and burns.

"Appetite suppressing eyeglasses" are common eyeglasses with colored lenses that claim to project an image to the retina which dampens the desire to eat. There is no evidence these work.

"Magic weight-loss earrings" and devices custom-fitted to the purchaser's ear that purport to stimulate acupuncture points controlling hunger have not been proven effective.

Diet Programs

Approximately 8 million Americans a year enroll in some kind of structured weight-loss program involving liquid diets, special diet regimens, or medical or other supervision. In 1991, about 8,500 commercial diet centers were in operation across the country, many of them owned by a half-dozen or so well-known national companies.

Before you join such a program, you should know that according to published studies relatively few participants succeed in keeping off weight *long-term*. Recently, the FTC brought action against several companies challenging weight-loss and weight-maintenance claims. Unfortunately, some other companies continue to make overblown claims.

The FTC stopped one company from claiming its diet program caused rapid weight loss through the use of tablets that would "burn fat" and a protein drink mix that would adjust metabolism. The FTC also took action against three major programs using doctor-supervised, very low-calorie liquid diets, and they agreed to stop making the claims they had been making unless they could back them up with hard data.

Before you sign up with a diet program, you might ask these questions:

What are the health risks?

What data can you show me that proves your program actually works?

Do customers keep off the weight after they leave the diet program?

What are the costs for membership, weekly fees, food, supplements, maintenance, and counseling?

What's the payment schedule? Are any costs covered under health insurance? Do you give refunds if I drop out?

Do you have a maintenance program? Is it part of the package or does it cost extra?

What kind of professional supervision is provided? What are the credentials of these professionals?

What are the program's requirements? Are there special menus or foods, counseling visits, or exercise plans?

Sensible Weight Maintenance Tips

Losing weight may not be effortless, but it doesn't have to be complicated. To achieve long-term results, it's best to avoid quick-fix schemes and complex regimens. Focus instead on making modest changes to your life's daily routine. A balanced, healthy diet and sensible, regular exercise are the keys to maintaining your ideal weight. Although nutrition science is constantly evolving, here are some generally-accepted guidelines for losing weight:

Consult with your doctor, a dietician, or other qualified health professional to determine your ideal healthy body weight.

Avoiding Marketplace Perils

Eat smaller portions and those from a variety of foods.

Load up on foods naturally high in fiber: fruits, vegetables, legumes, and whole grains.

Limit portions of foods high in fat: dairy products like cheese, butter, and whole milk; red meat; cakes and pastries.

Exercise at least three times a week.

For Help and Information

The Federal Trade Commission has jurisdiction over the advertising and marketing of foods, non-prescription drugs, medical devices, and health care services. The FTC can seek federal court injunctions to halt fraudulent claims and obtain redress for injured consumers.

The Food and Drug Administration has jurisdiction over the content and labeling of foods, drugs, and medical devices. The FDA can take law enforcement action to seize and prohibit the sale of products that are falsely labeled.

Most state Attorneys General have authority under state consumer protection statutes to investigate and prosecute unfair or deceptive acts and practices. Many have the power to seek consumer restitution, civil fines, and revocation of a company's authority to do business.

To get more information or to file complaints about weight-loss products or programs, write:

Federal Trade Commission
Correspondence Branch
Washington, D.C. 20580 or

Food and Drug Administration
Consumer Affairs and Information
5600 Fishers Lane, HFC-110
Rockville, MD 20857 or

Your State Attorney General
Office of Consumer Protection
Your State Capital

[*Reprinted from a pamphlet published by the FTC, Food and Drug Administration, and the National Association of Attorneys General.]

DO YOU SPEAK "PENSIONESE"? HERE'S SOME HELP...*

Understanding the language is an important part of exploring the pension universe. If you understand the terms used by pension plan administrators and their booklets, you can better understand the way pensions work. The following are some commonly used pension terms:

Annuity: Pension benefits may be paid in different ways. One method of payment is an *annuity*. An *annuity* provides income for a specified period of time, such as a number of years or for life. One who receives payments under an *annuity* is an annuitant.

Break in Service: When a fulltime employee works 500 hours or less during a one-year period, a *break in service* has occurred. The pension plan rules on *break in service* determine how this affects the vesting for the employee once he or she returns to work.

Cash Out: When you leave a job before retirement, the amount of benefit you have earned in your pension may be *cashed out* to you by your employer. This is done by your employer making a lump sum distribution to you, called a *cash out*, thus closing your pension account.

Defined-Benefit Plan: This is a common type of pension plan under which a certain pension amount is promised to you by your employer based on a definite formula. This formula may provide that your benefit will be a particular percentage of your average pay over your entire service or over a particular number of years; it may provide for a flat monthly payment; or it may provide a definite amount for each year of service, expressed either as a percentage of pay or as a flat dollar amount for each year of service. You know what you can count on for your pension income under a *defined-benefit plan*. The employer usually pays into such a plan without deducting anything from your earnings.

Defined Contribution Plan: This is another common type of pension plan under which set payments or *contributions* are made for each employee and set aside in individual accounts for retirement. *Contributions* may come out of your earnings, matched by the employer. Alternatively, the employer may pay a major share or all of it. It is not known exactly what the benefit will be upon retirement since it depends on how much is accumulated in contributions and how well the money has been invested and managed by the employer.

Employee Retirement Income Security Act of 1974 (ERISA): This Act, signed into law in 1974, regulates the majority of private pension and welfare group plans in the U.S. It sets requirements for participation, vesting and other areas of pension practices.

Individual Retirement Account (IRA): The *IRA* is very much like a savings account but is designed specifically for accumulating retirement income. It is not set up or sponsored by an employer like pension plans. An individual may set aside retirement money in an *IRA* while enjoying the benefit of tax deductions, within specified limits.

Avoiding Marketplace Perils

Integration: Some employers take the Social Security benefits you have earned into account when figuring out your pension benefit. In other words, they *integrate* Social Security benefits with pension benefits. In effect, when employers practice *integration* they subtract from your earned pension benefit a percentage of your Social Security benefit. For the low income wage earner, this may significantly reduce the pension or cancel it out altogether.

Joint and Survivor Benefit: When a pension plan provides retirement benefits to a married person, it must also provide for a husband and wife pension or a *joint and survivor benefit*. This means that, as the spouse of a participant, you may receive a survivor benefit in the event of your spouse's death. The *joint and survivor benefit* would be at least one-half the amount your spouse would receive while still living. You can revoke this survivor benefit in exchange for higher benefits while your spouse is living but only by signing a statement witnessed by a Notary Public or pension plan administrator. You are entitled to a *joint and survivor benefit* even if your worker spouse dies before reaching retirement age as long as your spouse is vested in the pension plan.

Participation: You must be an official member or *participant* in a pension plan before you begin to add up, or accrue, benefits. To be eligible for *participation* in most pension plans, you must be at least 21 years of age and have worked for your employer for a specified period of time.

Portability: This term is used to describe the capacity to take accumulated monies in your pension fund with you when moving from one employer to another. A *portable* pension can be carried with you from job to job.

Private Pension Plan: Pension plans established by nongovernmental employers are classified as *private pension plans*.

Public Pension Plan: Pension plans offered to government employees by city, county, state and federal governments are *public pension plans*.

Vesting: The process of vesting a pension is basically that of earning a nonforfeitable right to the money in your pension fund. Once you are *vested* in a pension plan you have an insured right to the benefits in the fund for your retirement. Your own contributions to your pension are always fully *vested*, but the contributions made by your employer are vested according to different formulas whereby it is *vested* in stages or all at once. Employers set different rates for vesting. Typically, you are fully vested after five years of participation.

[*Reprinted from *The OWL Observer Newspaper*, 1985, published by the Older Women's League, 666 11th Street, N.W., Washington, D.C. 20001.]

Why Women Pay More

IF YOU SUSPECT CREDIT DISCRIMINATION...*

The law says that when creditors report histories to credit bureaus or to other creditors they must report information on accounts shared by married couples in both names. This is true only for accounts opened after June 1, 1977. If you and your spouse opened an account before that time, you should ask the creditor to use both names.

If you are married, divorced, separated, or widowed, you should make a special point to call or visit your local credit bureau(s) ensure that all relevant information in is a file under your own name. To learn more about building your credit file, write for a free brochure, "Women and Credit Histories," from any of the FTC offices listed below.

What You Can Do If You Suspect Discrimination

* Complain to the creditor. Make it known that your are aware of the law. The creditor may reverse the decision or detect an error.

* Many states have their own equal credit opportunity laws. Check with your state's Attorney General's office to see if the creditor violated state laws. Your state may decide to take the creditor to court.

* Bring a case in Federal District court. If you win, you can recover your damages and be awarded a penalty. You can also recover reasonable attorney's fees and court costs. An attorney can advise you on how to proceed.

* Join with others to file a class action suit. You may recover punitive damages for the class of up to $500,000 or 1 percent of the creditor's net worth, whichever is less.

* Report violations to the appropriate government agency. If you are denied credit, the creditor must give you the name and address of the agency to contact. While the agencies do not resolve individual complaints, they do use consumer comments to decide which companies to investigate. A list of agencies is listed below.

Where To Send Complaints and Questions

If retail store, department store, small loan and finance company, mortgage company, oil company, public utility company, state credit union, government lending program or travel and expense credit card company is involved, contact the Federal Trade Commission office nearest you:

1718 Peachtree Street, N.W., Suite 1000
Atlanta, Georgia 30367
(404) 347-4836

10 Causeway Street, Suite 1184
Boston, Massachusetts 02222
(617) 565-7240

55 East Monroe Street, Suite 1437
Chicago, Illinois 60603
(312) 353-4423

668 Euclid Avenue, Suite 520-A
Cleveland, Ohio 44114
(216) 522-4210

100 N. Central Expressway, Suite 500
Dallas, Texas 75201
(214) 767-5501

1405 Curtis Street, Suite 2900
Denver, Colorado 80202-2393
(303) 844-2271

11000 Wilshire Boulevard, Suite 13209
Los Angeles, California 90024
(213) 209-7890

150 William Street, 13th Floor
New York, New York 10038
(212) 264-1207

901 Market Street, Suite 570
San Francisco, California 94103
(415) 744-7920

915 Second Avenue, Suite 2806
Seattle, Washington 98174
(206) 442-4656

FTC HEADQUARTERS
Federal Trade Commission
6th & Pennsylvania Avenue, N.W.
Washington, D.C 20580
(202) 326-2222
TDD (202) 326-2502

* If your complaint concerns a nationally-chartered bank (National or N.A. will be part of the name), write to:

> Comptroller of Currency
> Consumer Affairs Division
> Washington, D.C. 20551

* If your complaint concerns a state-chartered bank and it is insured by the Federal Deposit Insurance Corporation, but is not a member of the Federal Reserve System, write to:

> FDIC
> Consumer Affairs Division
> Washington, D.C. 20429

* If your complaint concerns a federally-chartered or federally-insured savings and loan association, write to:

> Consumer Affairs Division
> Office of Thrift Supervision
> Washington, D.C. 20552

* If your complaint concerns a federally-chartered credit union, write to:

> National Credit Union Administration
> Consumer Affairs Division
> Washington, D.C. 20458

* Complaints against all kinds of creditors can be referred to:

> Department of Justice
> Civil Rights Division
> Washington, D.C. 20530

[*Reprinted from Federal Trade Commission's Fact Sheet on Credit Discrimination, FTC, Washington, D.C. 20580]

Avoiding Marketplace Perils

BILL OF RIGHTS FOR DIVORCE CLIENTS*

1. You have a right to discuss the proposed rates and retainer fee with your lawyer and you have the right to bargain about the fees before you sign the agreement as in any other contract.

2. You have the right to know how many attorneys and other legal staff will be working on your case at any given time, and what you will be charged for their services.

3. You have the right to know in advance how you will be asked to pay legal fees and expenses at the end of the case. If you pay for a retainer, you may ask reasonable questions about how the money will be spent or has been spent and how much of it remains unspent.

4. You are under no legal obligation to sign a Confession of Judgment or Promissory Note, or agree to a lien or mortgage on your home to cover legal fees. You are under no legal obligation to waive your rights to dispute a bill for legal services.

5. You have a right to a reasonable estimate of future necessary costs. If your lawyer agrees to lend or advance you money for preparing your case, you have the right to know periodically how much money your lawyer has spent on your behalf. You also have the right to decide, after consulting with your lawyer, how much money is to be spent to prepare a case. If you pay the expenses, you have the right to decide how much to spend.

6. You have the right to ask your lawyer at reasonable intervals how the case is

progressing and to have these questions answered to the best of your lawyer's ability.

7. You have the right to make the final decision regarding the settlement of your case.

8. You have a right to any original documents that are part of your attorney's work product. For instance, if you gave your present attorney documents from another attorney, you have a right to those documents. You have a right to ask your attorney to forward documents to you in a timely manner as he/she receives them from your spouse's attorney.

9. You have a right to be present at court conferences relating to your case that are held with judges and attorneys, and you also have the right to bring a family member or a friend to all court proceedings, unless a judge orders otherwise.

10. You have the right to know the cost of bringing a motion. The case may vary depending on the lawyer's rates and circumstances of the case, but you have the right to a general estimate.

If at any time, you, the client, believe that your lawyer has charged an excessive or illegal fee, you have the right to report the matter to a disciplinary or grievance committee that oversees lawyer misconduct.
[* Prepared by the New York City Department of Consumer Affairs, 42 Broadway, New York, NY 19994 (212) 487-4444.]

Why Women Pay More

CANADIAN ADVERTISING FOUNDATION
SEX-ROLE
STEREOTYPING GUIDELINES

GUIDELINES

The intent of these guidelines is to encourage advertising in all media to portray women and men in a manner which reflects their emotional and intellectual equality and which respects their equal dignity.

1. AUTHORITY

Advertising should take steps to attain significant positive change in the balance of women and men in roles of authority such as announcers, voiceovers, experts and on-camera authorities.

Comment

Research conducted on broadcast advertising in 1984 revealed a heavy imbalance in the number of male versus female voiceovers, as well as in roles of experts and product/service authorities. Further, no data could be found to provide greater effectiveness of males in these roles.

This area of advertising remains a male-dominated bastion because of the pool of extensively trained male voices exceeds the availability of female voices with comparable backgrounds in radio announcing or other equivalent training. The advertising industry should work toward correcting this imbalance and encourage the promotion of demonstration tapes and lists of female talent to the industry to facilitate positive change in the use of women these roles.

2. SEXUALITY

Advertising should avoid exploiting sexuality.

Comment

Exploiting is interpreted as a presentation in which sexuality is on display merely for the gratification of others. Some examples of exploitative uses are double entendres, camera as voyeur, unnatural physical positions, etc.

There is, however, nothing wrong with tasteful, positive, relevant sexuality in advertising which portrays a person in control of and celebrating her/his own sexuality.

3. DECISION-MAKING

Both women and men should be portrayed as decision-makers, particularly as buyers and users of big-ticket items and major services, as well as smaller purchases.

Comment

Both women and men are active decision-makers for major personal and household purchases and in the workforce. Decisions on life insurance, cars, major appliances, office equipment and systems, travel, etc. are often team decisions — whether in the workplace or at home. Many women make major purchasing decisions on their own and many men are frequently the purchasers of household items, grocery and drug products.

4. HOUSEHOLD

Males and females should be portrayed as equally sharing and benefiting from household management and tasks.

Comment

Canadians live in a variety of household arrangements and this should be reflected in advertising. Advertising should portray home management — organizing, care-giving, decision-making — as a shared responsibility of members of a unit and give equal dignity to domestic and wage-earning roles.

Non-traditional households, e.g., childless couples, single parent families, "empty nesters," etc., are all important purchasing units and should be used in advertising as well as the more traditional family unit.

5. DIVERSITY

Women and men in a variety of ages, backgrounds and appearances should both be portrayed in a wide range of contemporary occupations, hobbies, activities and interests.

Comment

Advertising should portray an expanded range of roles for both women and men reflecting more accurately contemporary Canadian society.

Women as doctors, politicians, parachutists, men as care-givers, computer operators, are lifestyles and occupational choices commonly seen in real life situations. Further, Canadians of all ages, appearances and backgrounds should be considered when creating advertising. The goal is to show a significant broadening in the diversity of characters and their assigned roles in advertising.

6. LANGUAGE

Advertising should use generic terms which include both sexes.

Comment

Language should be used which recognizes the equal treatment of women and men and does not exclude one sex, provided these terms have common understanding in vocabulary across the country. Contemporary Canadian language is changing and now includes terms in common usage such as Business Executive and Firefighter in place of Businessman and Fireman. Advertising should reflect this.

BACKGROUND

Sex-role stereotyping guidelines were originally developed by a Canadian Radio-television and Telecommunications Commission Task Force on Sex-role Stereotyping in the Broadcast Media in 1981. They have been administered by the Canadian Advertising Foundation since then and applied to all media.

The revised guidelines (dated 24 July 1987) were developed in 1987 through a consultation process with the advertising industry and public representatives. They are administered by the Canadian Advertising Foundation through French and English Advisory Panels on Sex-role Stereotyping.

These guidelines represent one important element of the Canadian advertising industry's commitment to self-regulation in the area of portrayal of women. Past experience has shown that self-regulation, involving industry and public representatives, has been effective in creating positive change and is more flexible and less costly to administer than government regulation.

The advertising industry collectively supports these guidelines and encourages all individual advertisers and agencies to reflect them in responsible, realistic and ultimately more effective advertising executions.

Complaints should be sent to:
Canadian Advertising Foundation, Advisory Division, 350 Bloor Street East, Suite 402, Toronto, Ontario M4W IH5 (416) 961-6311.

Avoiding Marketplace Perils

REGULATING COSMETICS*

The U.S. Food, Drug and Cosmetic Act defines cosmetics as "articles other than soap which are applied to the human body for cleansing, beautifying, promoting attractiveness or altering the appearance."

FDA has classified cosmetics into 13 categories:

- skin care (creams, lotions, powders, and sprays)
- fragrances
- eye makeup
- manicure products
- makeup other than eye (e.g., lipstick, foundation and blush)
- hair coloring preparations
- shampoos, permanent waves and other hair products
- deodorants
- shaving products
- baby products (e.g., shampoos, lotions and powders)
- bath oils and bubble baths
- mouthwashes
- sunscreens

It is against the law to distribute cosmetics that contain poisonous or harmful substances that might injure users under normal conditions. Manufacturing or holding cosmetics under unsanitary conditions, using non-permitted colors or including any filthy, putrid or decomposed substance is also illegal.

Except for color additives and a few prohibited ingredients, a cosmetic manufacturer may use any ingredient or raw material and market the final product without government approval. The prohibited ingredients are:

- biothionol
- hexachlorophene
- mercury compounds (except as preservatives in eye cosmetics)
- vinyl chloride and zirconium salts in aerosol products
- halogenated salicylanilides
- chloroform
- methylene chloride

Manufacturers must test color additives for safety and gain FDA approval for their intended use.

Why Women Pay More

Cosmetic firms may voluntarily register their manufacturing plants with FDA, file cosmetic formulas and report adverse reactions.

Cosmetic labels must list ingredients in descending order of predominance.

Trade secrets (as defined by FDA) and the ingredients of flavors and fragrances do not have to be specifically listed.

[*Reprinted from "Cosmetic Safety: More Complex than at First Blush," *FDA Consumer*, November, 1991.]

Beauty on the Safe Side*

Besides never putting on makeup while driving, consumers should follow other precautions to protect themselves and the quality of their cosmetics:

■ Keep makeup containers tightly closed except when in use.

■ Keep makeup out of sunlight; light can degrade preservatives.

■ Don't use eye cosmetics if you have an eye infection, such as conjunctivitis, and throw away all products you were using when you first discovered the infection.

■ Never add any liquid to bring the product back to its original consistency. Adding water or, even worse, saliva could introduce bacteria that could easily grow out of control. "If it has lost its original texture and consistency," says Gerald McEwen, Ph.D., of the Cosmetic, Toiletry and Fragrance Association, "the preservatives have probably broken down."

■ Never share.

■ Throw makeup away if the color changes or an odor develops. Preservatives can degrade over time and may no longer be able to fight bacteria.

"We don't have a hard and fast rule on [when to throw cosmetics out]," says McEwen. He says makeup can be kept indefinitely as long as it looks and smells all right and the consistency doesn't change. "It would be difficult to have any kind of bacterial growth and not have it be noticeable," McEwen explains.

Avoiding Marketplace Perils

However, Janice Teal, a microbiologist who heads the product and package safety division of Avon Products, Inc., disagrees. "Even after the preservatives have stopped working, you may not be able to see or smell anything different," she says.

She agrees with McEwen that there is no absolute date for discarding various products, but says Avon recommends that consumer throw mascara away after three months. They can keep other makeup products a few months longer.

"Mascara is our biggest concern because of the wand." she says. "Normally, the eye is a good barrier to bacteria, but one slip and that wand can scratch the cornea and introduce all kinds of bacteria."

[*Reprinted from "Cosmetic Safety: More Complex than at First Blush," *FDA Consumer*, November, 1991.]

Why Women Pay More

Notes

In The Market

1. *Gypped By Gender* (New York: New York City Department of Consumer Affairs, June 1992) p. 1.

2. Dale Fuchs, "Repairing Auto Laws," *Newsday*, December 9, 1992, p. 27.

3. "Hurricanes Blow Sears Profits", *Chicago Tribune*, October 22, 1992, p. 1.

4. Fuchs, p. 27.

5. "Carbriefs," *Gannett News Service*, November 3, 1992.

6. Warren Brown, "Who Gets the Best Deals on Wheels?" *The Washington Post*, December 14, 1990, p. F1.

7. Brown, p. 2.

8. Rhona Mahoney, "Driving Hard Bargains," *The Guardian*, January 29, 1992.

9. *Gypped by Gender.*

10. *Gypped by Gender.*

11. "Women Pay More For Services, Survey Says," *UPI*, June 4, 1992.

12. Joanne Ball Artis, "Combatting Gender Bias at the Hair Salon," *The Boston Globe*, December 19, 1992, p. 27.

13. Artis, p. 27.

14. *Gypped by Gender*, pp. 3-4.

15. Davan Maharaj, "Alteration Altercation," *The Los Angeles Times*, August 9, 1989, Part 4, p. 1.

16. "Auto Repairs," *Washington Consumers' Checkbook* (Washington, D.C.: Center for Study of Consumer Services, Winter/Spring 1991), pp. 16-17.

Health Chapter

1. I. Ray, *Mental Hygiene* (New York: Hafner Publishing Company, 1968 [facsimile of 1863 edition]), p. 54.

2. "Gender Disparities in Clinical Decision Making," Report by the Council on Ethical and Judicial Affairs, American Medical Association, *Journal of the American Medical Association*, July 24, 1991.

3. "Gender Disparities in Clinical Decision Making."

4. "Deaths, by Age and Leading Causes: 1989," *Statistical Abstract of the United States,* 112th edition (Washington, D.C.: U.S. Bureau of the Census, 1992, No. 116), p. 84.

5. "Gender Disparities in Clinical Decision Making."

6. *The New York Times*, October 19, 1992, p. 15.

7. Robin Herman, "What Doctors Don't Know About Women," *The Washington Post*, December 8, 1992, Health Section.

8. "Women's Health Issues Take Center Stage at the IOM," *Science*, October 30, 1992.

9. Debra Roter, Mack Lipkin, and Audrey Korsagaard, "Sex Differences in Patients' and Physicians' Communications During Primary

Care Medical Visits," *Medical Care*, Vol. 29, No. 11, November 1991.

10. "Employed Civilians, by Occupation, Sex, Race and Hispanic Origin: 1983 and 1991," *Satistical Abstract of the United States,* 112th edition (Washington, D.C.: U.S. Bureau of the Census, 1992, No. 629), p. 392.

11. "Gender Disparities in Clinical Decision Making."

12. N.K. Wenger, "Coronary Disease in Women," Ann Rev Med. 1985; 36:285-294, cited in "Gender Disparities in Clinical Decision Making," *Journal of the American Medical Association*, July 24, 1991.

13. Sidney M. Wolfe, *Women's Health Alert* (New York: Addison-Wesley, 1991), p. 146.

14. *Women's Dependency on Prescription Drugs*, Hearings before the Select Committee on Narcotics Abuse & Control (Washington, D.C.: U.S. House of Representatives, September 13, 1979), pp. 4-19.

15. Wolfe, p. 153.

16. Wolfe, p. 146.

17. Wolfe, p. 161.

18. Wolfe, p. 120.

19. Wolfe, p. 194.

20. Wolfe, p. 194.

21. Wolfe, p. 207.

22. Wolfe, p. 223.

23. Wolfe, p. 224.

24. "In Vitro Fertilization - Embryo Transfer (IVF-ET) in the United States: 1990 Results from the IVF-ET Registry," *Fertility and Sterility*, Vol. 57, No. 1, January 1992.

25. Wolfe, p. 22.

26. "Silicone Gel Implants Cause Cancer," *Health Letter* (Washington, D.C.: Public Citizen Health Research Group, December 1988).

27. "Silicone Gel Implants Cause Cancer."

28. Wolfe, p. 27.

29. *Information on Breast Implant Litigation* fact sheet (Washington, D.C.: Public Citizen Health Research Group).

30. Wolfe, p. 46.

31. Wolfe, p. 48.

32. Wolfe, p. 47.

33. "Cesarean Section Deliveries, by Age of Mother: 1970-1989," *Statistical Abstract of the United States*, 112 edition (Washington, D.C.: U.S. Bureau of the Census, 1992, No. 86), p. 67.

34. Dale A. Tussing and Martha Wojtowycz, "The Cesarian Decision in New York State, 1986," *Medical Care*, Vol. 30, No. 6, June 1992, p. 532.

35. Tussing and Wojtowycs, p. 532.

36. Tussing and Wojtowycs, p. 533.

37. Tussing and Wojtowycs, p. 529.

38. Tussing and Wojtowycs, p. 539.

39. Wolfe, p. 73.

40. Linda V. Walsh, *Midwife, An Historical Perspective*, brochure to accompany an exhibition on the History of Midwifery, (Washington, D.C.: American College of Nurse-Midwives, 1991).

41. Eugene R. Declercq, "The Transformation of American Midwifery: 1975-1988," *American Journal of Public Health*, Vol. 82, No. 3, May 1992, p. 683.

42. The Boston Women's Health Book Collective, *The New Our Bodies, Ourselves* (New York: Touchstone, 1992) p. 412.

43. Kathleen Kelleher, "Women at Risk," *The Los Angeles Times*, November 11, 1992, p. 7C.

44. Bernadine Healy, "Rx for Women's Better Health," *USA Today*, September, 16, 1992, p. 15A.

45. B.D. Colen, "AIDS Warning: Peril Looms For Women, Experts Say," *Newsday*, July 21, 1992, p. 3.

46. David Perlman, "The Gender Gap In AIDS Diagnosis," *The San Francisco Chronicle*, June 20, 1992, p. A2.

47. Kelleher, p. 7C.

48. Roni Rabin, "Turning Away Women with AIDS," *Newsday*, February 15, 1993, p.16.

49. Joan E. Rigdon, "Saline Implants Appear to Carry Hazards As Well," *The Wall Street Journal*, February 4, 1993, p. B10.

Finance Chapter

1. *Mothers, Children and Low-Wage Work: the Ability to Earn a Family Wage* fact sheet (Washington, D.C.: Institute for Women's Policy Research, 1991).

2. *Mothers, Children and Low-Wage Work...*

3. *Are Mommies Dropping out of the Labor Force?* fact sheet (Washington, D.C.: Institute for Women's Policy Research, 1992).

4. "Heading for Hardship: Retirement Income for American Women in the Next Century," *Mother's Day Report* (Washington, D.C.: Older Women's League, 1990), p. 1.

5. Press Release (Washington, D.C.: Federal Trade Commission, February 2, 1990).

6. Press Release (Washington, D.C.: Federal Trade Commission, July 12, 1990).

7. Ginita Wall, *Our Money Our Selves* (Yonkers, NY: Consumers Union, 1992), pp. 43-44.

8. *Equal Credit Opportunity* pamphlet (Washington, D.C.: Federal Trade Commission).

9. Gayle Melich, National Women's Political Caucus, Testimony on Sex Discrimination in Insurance before the Senate Commerce, Science and Transportation Committee, July 15, 1982.

10. Patrick Butler and Twiss Butler, "Sex-Divided Mileage, Accident and Insurance Cost Data Show That Auto Insurers Overcharge most Women," *Journal of Insurance Regulation*, Vol. 6, No.3, March 1988, p. 243.

11. Judy Goldsmith, National Organization for Women, Testimony on the Equal Rights Amendment before the Subcommittee on Civil and Constitutional Rights of the House Committee on the Judiciary, September 14, 1983.

12. Butler, Butler and Williams, p. 245.

13. The Insurance Project, National Organization for Women, testimony "Pregnancy

Discrimination in Health Insurance," before the Pennsylvania NOW Issues Conference, August 3, 1991.

14. Carolyn M. Clancy and Charlea T. Massion, "American Women's Health Care," *Journal of the American Medical Association*, October 4, 1992, p. 191.

15. Clancy and Massion, p. 191.

16. Clancy and Massion, p. 191.

17. Memo from Karen Scott Collins, MD, M.P.H., Johns Hopkins University School of Public Health, December 14, 1992.

18."Heading for Hardship: Retirement for American Women in the Next Century."

19."Heading for Harship..."

20. Frances Leonard, *Women & Money* (New York: Addison-Wesley, 1991), p. 144.

21. "Current Population Survey," March 1987, cited in *Legal Resource Kit*, (New York: NOW Legal Defense & Education Fund, 1988).

22. *Legal Resource Kit.*

23. "Heading for Hardship..."

24. *Legal Resource Kit*, p. 6.

Legal Chapter

1. Frances Leonard, *Women & Money* (New York: Addison-Wesley, 1991), p. 25.

2. *Women in Divorce* (New York: New York City Department of Consumer Affairs, March 1992), p. 18.

3. *Women in Divorce*, p. 8.

4. *Gender, Justice & the Courts*, Report of the Connecticut Task Force (Hartford, CT: 1991), p. 32.

5. "Child Support and Alimony: 1989" *Current Population Reports* (Washington, D.C.: U.S. Bureau of the Census, Series P-60, No. 173), p. 12.

6. *Gray Paper, Divorce and Older Women* (Washington, D.C.: Older Women's League, 1988) p. 4.

7. *Women in Divorce*, p. 8.

8. Leonard, p. 11.

9. Leonard, p. 13.

10. *Gray Paper, Divorce and Older Women*, p. 5.

11. *Women in Divorce*, p. 39.

12. *Women in Divorce*, p. 39.

13. *Women in Divorce*, p. 35.

14. Susan Freinkel, "Breaking Up is Hard to do," *American Lawyer*, November 2, 1992, p. 1.

15. *Woman in Divorce*, p. 9.

16. *Gray Paper, Divorce and Older Women*, p. 8.

17. *Women in Divorce*, p. 9.

18. *Model Rules of Professional Conduct* (Chicago, IL: American Bar Association, 1992), Rule 6.1.

19. *Gray Paper, Divorce and Older Women*, p. 9.

20. "Anita Hill Urges Women Judges to Rush for a Change," *Associate Press, The Los Angeles Times*, October 10, 1992, p. B3.

21. John M. O'Connell, "Keeping Sex Out of the Attorney-Client Relationship; A Proposed Rule," *Columbia Law Review*, May, 1992.

22. *Gender, Justice and the Courts*, p. 124.

23. *Gender, Justice and the Courts*, p. 140.

24. "Earned Degrees Conferred," *Statistical Abstract of the United States*, 112 edition (Washington, D.C.: U.S. Bureau of the Census, 1992, No. 279), p. 173.

25. *Gender Bias Study of the Supreme Judicial Court, Commonwealth of Massachusetts*, (Boston: 1989), p. 39.

26. L. Woods, V. Been and J. Schulman, *The Use of Sex and Economic Discriminatory Criteria in Child Custody Awards* (New York: National Center for Women and Family Law, 1982).

27. Woods, Been and Schulman.

28. Woods, Been and Schulman.

29. *Gender Bias Study...*, p. 59.

30. "Friendly Parent Provisions in Custody Determinations," *The Women's Advocate*, (New York: National Center on Women and Family Law, Vol. 13, No. 5, September 1992), pp. 1-2.

31. Sheila Weller, "Abused by the Courts," *The Village Voice*, December 1, 1992, p. 1.

32. Weller, p. 1.

33. "Friendly Parent..." p. 2.

34. *Gender Bias Study...*, p. 59.

35. *Alternatives Newsletter* (New York: National Center for Protective Parents, Vol. 1, No. 1, Fall 1992), p. 1.

36. "Child Support Enforcement," *Fifteenth Annual Report to Congress by the Office of Child Support Enforcement* (Washington, D.C.: U.S. Department of Health & Human Services, 1990), p. 5.

37. Jeanne L. Reid, "Making Delinquent Dad Pay His Child Support," *Ms.*, July/August, 1992, pp. 86-87.

38. *Childhood's End: What Happens to Children When Child Support Obligations Are Not Enforced* (Uniondale, NY: The National Child Support Assurance Consortium, The Health & Welfare Council, January 1993) p.11.

39. "Child Support and Alimony, 1989," *Current Population Reports* (Washington, D.C.: U.S. Bureau of Census), p.1.

40. "Friendly Parent," p. 2.

41. *Bradley v. State of Mississippi*, (Walker) 156, 158 (1824).

42. William Prosser, *Handbook of The Law of Torts*, (St. Paul, MN: West Publishing Co., 4th Edition, 1971), p. 136.

43. *Violence Against Women* fact sheet (Washington, D.C.: Congressional Caucus for Women's Issues, October 1992), p. 6.

44. *Violence Against Women*, p. 7.

45. Joanne Schulman, *Poor Women and Family Law* (New York: National Center for Women and Family Law, 1982), p. 3.

46. "Three Analyses of the Effects of Arrest for Domestic Violence," *American Sociological Review*, Volume 57, No. 5, October 1992.

47. "Divorce & Annulments - Median Duration of Marriage, 1970-1988," *Statistical Abstract of the United States: 1992*, 112th edition (Washington, D.C.: U.S. Bureau of the Census, 1992, No. 132), p. 92.

Advertising

1. John Berger, *Ways of Seeing* (London: Penguin, 1972), p. 134.

2. Stuart Ewen, *Captains of Consciousness* (New York: McGraw-Hill 1976), p. 153.

3. Gretchen Metzger, "TV Is a Blonde, Blonde, World," *American Demographics*, November 1992, p. 51.

4. Connie Danese, "SAG Conference Addresses and Denounces Female Struggles in Film and TV," *Back Stage*, August 17, 1990, p. 3.

5. Danese, p. 3.

6. Diane Crispell, "The Brave New World of Men," *American Demographics*, January 1992, p. 38.

7. Sidney M. Wolfe, *Women's Health Alert* (New York: Addison-Wesley, 1991), p. 229.

8. Cited in *Nutrition Action Newsletter* (Washington, D.C.: Center for Science in the Public Interest, September 1992), p. 4.

9. "FTC Charges Marketers of Ultrafast, Medifast and Optifast Liquid Diet Programs," Press Release (Washington, D.C.: Federal Trade Commission, October 16, 1991).

10. Marian Burros, "U.S. Will Require New Labels on Health on Packaged Foods," *The New York Times*, December 3, 1992, p. A1.

11. "Cosmetics Regulations," *GAO Report to the Chairman*, Subcommittee on Regulation, Committee on Small Business, U.S. House of Representatives, (Washington, D.C.: General Accounting Office, March 1990).

12. "Shampoos," *Consumer Reports*, February 1989, pp. 95-99.

13. "Facial Cleansers," *Consumer Reports*, June, 1989, pp. 408-410.

14. Naomi Wolf, *The Beauty Myth* (New York: Doubleday, 1991), p. 77.

15. Gloria Steinem, "Sex, Lies & Advertising," *Ms.*, July/August 1990, p. 19.

16. K.E. Warner, L.M. Goldenhar, and C.G. McLaughlin, "Cigarette Advertising & Magazine Coverage," *The New England Journal of Medicine*, January 30, 1992, p. 305.

17. Warner, Goldenhar and McLaughlin, p. 305.

18. Warner, Goldenhar and McLaughlin, p. 308.

19. Data from the National Health Interview Study, (Washington, D.C.: National Center for Health Statistics, Division of Health Interview Statistics, 1991).

20. Phyllis L. Pirie, David M. Murray and Russell V. Luephen, "Gender Differences in Cigarette Smoking and Quitting," *American Journal of Public Health*, Vol. 81, No. 3, March 1991, pp. 325-326.

21. Jean Kilbourne, "Ads Teach Teens Dangerous Gender Stereotypes," *Advice* (Washington, D.C.: Center for the Study of Commercialism, Vol. 1, No. 4, January 1992).

22. Valeria Salember, "There Are Sexy Ads-and Sexist Ones," *Chicago Tribune*, October 18, 1992, WomaNews, p. 11.

23. Cyndee Miller, "Publisher says sexy ads are OK, but sexist ones will sink sales," *Marketing News*, November 23, 1992, p. 8.

24. Fred Pelka, "Dreamworlds," *On the Issues*, Vol. XXI, Winter 1991, pp. 24-39.

25. Pelka, p. 41.

26. Larry Fruhling, "Female Brewery Workers Fight Bimbo Commercials," *Gannett News Service*, November 30, 1992.

27. Ronald K.L. Collins, "Bikini Team: Sexism for the Many," *The Los Angeles Times*, November 20, 1991, p. B5.

28. Berger, p. 131.

29. Kathy Brown, "A Little Older, A Little Wiser," *Adweek*, June 22, 1992, p. 32.

30. "Sexy or Sexist? Recent Ads Spur Debate," *The Wall Street Journal*, Sept. 30, 1991, p. B1.

Fashion Chapter

1. Naomi Wolf, *The Beauty Myth* (New York: Doubleday, 1991), p. 10.

2. Marsha Richins, "Social Comparison and the Idealized Images of Advertising," *The Journal of Consumer Research*, June, 1991.

3. John Molloy, *The Women's Dress for Success Book* (New York: Warner Books, 1977).

4. *Thirty Five Million: The Status of Young Women*, (Washington, D.C.: Institute for Women's Policy Research, October 1990).

5. cited from *Apparel Industry Topline: January - September 1990/91/92* (Stamford, CT: MRCA Information Services, November 6, 1992).

6. "How to Judge a Suit," *Consumer Reports*, September 1992, p. 563.

7. Wolf, p. 207.

8. Frances Grandy Taylor, "Strategies for Putting on the Best Face," *The Hartford Courant*, September 14, 1991, p. B1.

9. "Facial Cleansers," *Consumer Reports*, June 1989, p. 409.

10. "Lipsticks," *Consumer Reports*, Feb, 1988, p. 76.

11. Dori Stehlin, "More Complex than at First Blush," *FDA Consumer*, November 1991.

12. Sidney M. Wolfe, *Women's Health Alert* (New York: Addison-Wesley, 1991), p. 249.

13. Wolfe, p. 253.

14. Germaine Greer, *The Change* (New York: Alfred A. Knopf, 1992).

15. Greer, p. 4.

16. Robert Scheer, "A Frenzy of Lifts, etc." *The Los Angeles Times*, Dec. 22, 1991, p. A1.

17. Scheer, p. A1.

18. *Is The FDA Protecting Consumers From Dangerous Off-label Uses of Medical Drugs and Devices?* Report by the House Committee on Government Operations, November, 1992, p. 7.

19. *Is the FDA Protecting Consumers...*, p. 21.

20. Greer, p. 238.